Violence

in Early Modernist Fiction:
The Secret Agent,
Tarr and
Women in Love

Izabela Curyłło-Klag

Violence

in Early Modernist Fiction:
The Secret Agent,
Tarr and
Women in Love

Jagiellonian University Press

The publication of this volume was supported by the Faculty of Philology of the Jagiellonian University.

Reviewer: prof. dr hab. Krystyna Stamirowska

Cover design and typesetting: Marcin Klag

Technical editor: Joanna Bernatowicz

ISBN 978-83-233-3232-9

www.wuj.pl

Jagiellonian University Press
ul. Michałowskiego 9/2, 31-126 Kraków
phone: (+48) 12-631-18-81, (+48) 12-631-18-82, fax: (+48) 12-631-18-83
Sales: phone: (+48) 12-631-01-97, phone/fax: (+48) 12-631-01-98
mobile: (+48) 506-006-674, e-mail: sprzedaz@wuj.pl
Bank account: PEKAO SA, nr 80 1240 4722 1111 0000 4856 3325

Contents

ACKNOWLEDGEMENTS

I am indebted to many people for their advice, help, and encouragement from the inception of this book to its present form, and I am delighted to express my gratitude to them here.

Since this study grew out of a doctoral thesis, I would like to thank my supervisor, Professor Krystyna Stamirowska, for her extraordinary patience, kindness, and understanding, in addition to her generous advice. I am also grateful to her for her reading of the manuscript in its entirety, shortly before its submission. My thanks are extended to the reviewers of the thesis, Professor Irena Przemecka and Professor Andrzej Weseliński, for their feedback and criticism.

I have also benefited from a visit to Royal Holloway, University of London, where I gathered material for my research. Professor Stephen Regan and Professor Robert Hampson made my visit not only fruitful and efficient but pleasant as well. Gratitude is also due to the staff of the Founder's Library for allowing me to explore their impressive collection of books and resources.

I am grateful to the English Department of the Jagiellonian University for their warm support in the crucial period of my work on this project. The staff of the Jagiellonian University English Department Library and the Jagiellonian Library deserve thanks for their patience and efficient response to my numerous requests.

Many of my friends and colleagues contributed in tangible and intangible ways to the completion of this book. Magdalena Bleinert and Ewa Kowal deserve thanks for their critical readings and constructive suggestions. Grażyna Branny and Aleksander Gomola have generously offered me access to their splendid collections of critical texts. I also wish to thank Katarzyna Bazarnik, Bożena Kucała, Robert Kusek, Grzegorz Szpila and Marcin Zydroń for their friendship and comic relief. Most of all, I am indebted to my husband Marcin for his unfailing devotion and intellectual stimulation, as well as for giving this book its cover and typographic shape.

One of the ways of approaching early modernist fiction is to view it as a record of catastrophic imagination. Shaped by the circumstances of its time—the excessive pace of civilisational advancement, ideological and ethical turmoil, the rise of militarism—it envisions dystopian scenarios and warns against a pandemonium that at any moment can ensue from the faltering system. A tremor runs through many modernist creations, investing them with "a sense of disorientation and nightmare"[1] which, according to Bradbury and McFarlane's standard definition, constitutes the hallmark of the epoch. Connected to this perpetual state of emergency is a constant anticipation of a violent breakthrough—some sudden, spasmodic occurrence that will radically put an end to what has deteriorated beyond repair. The forms of imagined violence are multiple, ranging from aberrant individual reversals to barbarity, threats of terrorism and foreign invasions, down to a universal collapse into the shambles of slaughter, or—perhaps more humane—a neat and quick self-annihilation by means of a perfect explosive.

In bringing together three important texts of British modernism, this book takes a closer look at such imaginings, and attempts to investigate them in the light of selected aspects of anthropological theory. It also takes into account the social and historical context in which they are grounded, for one of the premises of this study is the idea that literature is a reflection of a cultural moment. What comes into focus is the tension between the violence mythos, that is, "a set of attitudes and beliefs about violence

---

1   Malcolm Bradbury, James McFarlane, eds. *Modernism: A Guide to European Literature, 1890-1930,* (London: Penguin, 1991), 26.

existing in a given culture,"[2] and the symbolic realisation of this mythos in a literary form. The questions that this analysis seeks to answer are as follows: "Why is violence an issue in the texts selected?," "What do they reveal about the discourses of violence prevalent at the time?," and, finally, "What version of the violence mythos do they attempt to propagate?." If, as Fredric Jameson observes, narratives are always "socially symbolic acts,"[3] then modernist representations of violence must also have been intended to bear a cultural significance. Studied from the perspective of almost a century, they may be valuable to us for the purpose of reassessing the past models in the light of our culture's engagement with present crises.

Selected from the extensive modernist corpus, Joseph Conrad's *The Secret Agent*, Wyndham Lewis's *Tarr* and D.H. Lawrence's *Women in Love* exemplify some trends in the fictional representation of violence during the historically charged period from the beginning of the twentieth century to the end of the First World War. Taken chronologically, they reveal an unfolding pattern, indicative of the growing intensity of the epoch in which violence so fervently imagined was assuming a real shape. Each of the novels is pervaded with a sense of crisis and each seems to toy with a possibility that civilisation might end, whether with a bang, or a whimper. This pessimistic scenario is often enacted symbolically through the figure of a violent individual whose life serves as a prediction of the general destructive and self-destructive drift.

Any discussion of violence is inevitably challenged by the problematic and still not fully explored character of this phenomenon. Prodigious literature notwithstanding, few unifying theories are available that could provide methodological instruments for a systematic analysis. Because this study focuses on texts produced by Western culture in one of its most turbulent moments, it seemed appropriate that the textual investigations undertaken here should build on the anthropological insights of René Girard. His exploration of the mechanisms triggering the dissolution of social order, and his idea of "sacrificial crisis" as a favourable environment for the spreading of violent impulses constitute a point of departure for piecing together a fuller picture of the relationship between modernist fiction and cultural history.

The study is in four chapters. The historical and critical context for the analysis of the novels is outlined in Chapter I, along with a definition of the violence mythos and an explication of the theoretical notions applied in the discussion. The remaining chapters deal with one novel each. Chapter II explores undercurrents of violence simmering in

---

2 Definition provided by Barbara Whitmer in *The Violence Mythos*, (New York: State University of New York Press, 1997), 1. For an explication of her ideas, see Chapter I, section: "The Violence Mythos of Modernism," 21-22.

3 Fredric Jameson, *The Political Unconscious: Narrative as a Socially Symbolic Act*, (London: Methuen, 1981), 20.

the murky world of *The Secret Agent,* not yet conscious of its own aggressive potential. Chapter III, devoted to a discussion of *Tarr*, focuses on Wyndham Lewis's case study of a violent personality and ways in which aggressiveness is construed as a form of contagion. Finally, Chapter IV analyses Lawrence's vision of a society thoroughly infected with violence and heading towards self-annihilation.

All textual references in this study are based on fairly recent editions of the three works, which may occasionally differ from older publications. In the case of Wyndham Lewis's *Tarr*, it is the 1918 version of the novel (in the 1996 edition by Paul O'Keeffe) that has been selected for analysis, rather than the post-World War I revision, dating from 1928. The earlier text better fits the temporal framework of the present project, although the revised version, reissued in 2010 by Scott W. Klein, may now be more popular with the general reader (the 1996 edition is already out of print). Citations from the three analysed novels are indicated in parentheses, with the following abbreviations: *TS* for *The Secret Agent*, *T* for *Tarr*, and *WL* for *Women in Love*. References to critical and theoretical studies are listed as footnotes at the bottom of relevant pages.

CHAPTER I

Modernist Consciousness of Crisis and the Emergent Violence Mythos

What happens to tragedy in the twentieth century is not that it dies, but that it mutates into modernism. For a major strain of modernism belabours a middle-class society with which it nevertheless remains complicit, castigating the spiritually derelict condition from the right rather than the left. Modernism, too, can be rancorously anti-democratic, stridently elitist, homesick for the primitive and archaic, in thrall to spiritual absolutes which spell the death of liberal enlightenment. And if modernism lends the tragic impulse a new lease of life, it is not least because of the return of mythology. In the late modern era, mythical destiny shows its face again in the guise of vast, anonymous forces—language, will, power, history, production, desire—which live us far more than we live them.

Terry Eagleton, *Sweet Violence*

Modernism as Sacrificial Crisis

A recurrent theme foregrounded in critical discussions of modernism is a sense of crisis engendered by the process of dissociation from the great truths of the past epochs and by the impossibility of constructing a new system of reference that would allow for an equally efficient grasp of reality. As a result of the excessive pace of civilisational advancement at the turn of the twentieth century, traditional assumptions about the meaning of existence, the nature of society and the destiny of humanity lost their binding character, leaving people in a state of epistemological and ethical confusion. Doubt was cast over the entire cultural logic of the West: supposedly natural or God-given laws were now perceived as human constructs and social conventions, what had been considered the workings of divine providence could now be explained as physical accidents, and the rational ego of the Enlightenment was dismissed as self-deluded. With the corrosion of old certainties, anguish and pessimism crept in, giving rise to a proliferation of unsettling diagnoses of the modern condition. Terms which came to describe the response to the experience of modernity—decadence, *anomie*, alienation, neurosis, shock of the new— signalled the extent to which the world had been thrown out of kilter.

Stressed so many times that it may seem exploited, crisis is one of the concepts that help to account for modernism's interest in violence. The collapse of the traditional value system and the inability to exert mental control over a rapidly changing reality must have engendered considerable frustration, especially when set against the crassly triumphalist discourse which accompanied the modernising process. On the one hand, the boundaries of cognition seemed to have been pushed forward—man was hailed a godlike creature capable of seeing through the illusions of the past and making all kinds of incredible discoveries—and, on the other, there was a constant sense of disorientation and disquietude, the impression that things are not what they seem on the surface and that veracity dwells in depths which the human mind cannot penetrate.[4] In the words of one critic, "modernism began with the assumption of a coherent individual who could assess real phenomena through scientific methods, and ended with the individual subject alienated from a phenomenological reality that, while it did exist, remained too complex and contradictory for mere human consciousness to access."[5] As a result, modern utopian dreams were usually marred by a dystopian streak, and systematic models aroused suspicion of underlying chaos. Realising that their powers of reasoning were compromised by the infinite complicatedness of the universe, people began anticipating a backlash of progress—a moment when the price of modernisation would have to be paid. New possibilities seemed inextricably tied to deep anxieties: a vision of humanity being swallowed up by some universal confusion enjoyed a considerable, even if morbid, appeal.

In anthropology, the context of crisis is seen as conducive to violence. It is a state of transition in which social ties become loosened, old values no longer apply while new ones have not yet been established, and there is an excess of negative energy that badly needs channelling. The threat of disintegration looms large, for a general disposition towards radical action intensifies: as one interpreter of Girard's theory points out, "when cultures fall apart they fall into violence, and when they revive themselves, they do so

---

4   The sense of radical uncertainty was exacerbated by the scientific explorations which pointed to the existence of unknown and unknowable worlds. Roentgen's discovery of X-rays, the Curies' work on radioactivity, Rutherford's model of the atom, Eistein's relativity theory, and Freud's notion of the subconscious undermined the reassuringly stable view of reality inherited from previous generations.

5   Steven Alan Carr, "Mass Murder, Modernity and the Alienated Gaze," in: Pomerance Murray, ed., *Cinema and Modernity*, (New Brunswick: Rutgers University Press, 2006), 58.

violently."[6] Throughout the ages, various analysts of the human condition have observed that reconstitutions of society are enacted in turmoil and achieved by drastic methods. In Hegel's dialectic, the spirit of history manifests itself through struggle: thesis and antithesis must clash to make a synthesis possible. For Nietzsche, one of modernity's main ideologues, violation of continuities was a necessary precondition for a creative act. Frazer, Durkheim and Freud all agreed that social contracts entail coercion and are founded on violence, and in 1940 Walter Benjamin expressed a very similar idea in his "Theses on the Philosophy of History," claiming that "there is no document of civilisation which is not at the same time a document of barbarism."[7] More contemporary thinkers also stress the role of violence in the creation and destruction of social orders, noting that all kinds of transition periods are marked by acute awareness of the threat of violent outbreaks.[8]

One modern theory of society, proposed by René Girard, uses the concept of "sacrificial crisis" to describe a situation when social models and hierarchies break down, creating an environment of chaos and potential destructiveness. Following Frazer and Durkheim, Girard distinguishes between the profane (random) violence and sacred (constitutive) violence, the latter serving the purpose of a braking mechanism to prevent the self-annihilation of communities in an apocalyptic bloodbath. Elements of sacred violence can be recognised in the myth and ritual of primitive tribes, in religion, in mourning and funeral rites, in any sacrifice that restores order to society, as well as in the legal systems of modern states. When the effectiveness of protective institutions and practices is waning, people are likely to get trapped in a spiral of transgressive behaviour culminating in pandemic mutual hostility. The only way to end this escalating process is by means of violence invested with sacred meaning, that is, through a collectively sanctioned, climactic violent event. According to Girard, human history consists of cycles of sacrificial crises and their solutions, though since the advent of modernity the ancient, mythic methods of containing violence have been increasingly difficult to implement.

Drawing on Girard's explanation of the origins of violence, this study proposes to view the pre-war times—the times when early modernist works were written—as a period of sacrificial crisis, with World War I marking an attempt, evidently not

---

6   Gil Bailie, *Violence Unveiled: Humanity at the Crossroads*, (New York: The Crossroad Publishing Company, 1997), 6.

7   Walter Benjamin, "Theses on the Philosophy of History," in: *Illuminations*, (New York: Schocken Books, 1988), 258.

8   See for example: Anthony Giddens, *The Nation-State and Violence* (Berkeley: University of California Press, 1987), Piotr Hoffman, *Violence in Modern Philosophy* (Chicago: University of Chicago Press, 1989), or two works by Terry Eagleton, *Sweet Violence* (Oxford: Blackwell Publishing, 2003) and *Holy Terror* (Oxford: Oxford University Press, 2005).

successful, at its resolution. The epoch seems to have been beset by many disquieting symptoms which fit the Girardian model and which, operating all at once, culminated in a cultural meltdown on an unprecedented scale. Extending the customary summation of modernism by the word "sacrificial" will yield a more nuanced perspective on the "narratives of rupture" produced by the epoch's major literary presences. It will also draw attention to fundamental ethical concerns that modernists were grappling with from within their turbulent milieu.

Girard's theory is applicable to the early modernist period due to the fact that the epoch was marked by an erosion of spiritual authority and a dissolution of the taken-for-granted value systems. The process had been initiated long before, with the advent of modernity as such in the late seventeenth century, and gained impetus in the second half of the nineteenth century after the publication of Darwin's *On the Origin of Species* and after Nietzsche's notorious proclamation of the death of God. These developments, combined with the legacy of Enlightenment humanism, caused a desacralisation of human perspectives, i.e. made people less likely to accept the "sacredness" of certain concepts, including the concept of sacred violence. The Nietzschean gesture of smashing the idols with a hammer forever deprived Western culture of the possibility of applying solutions sanctioned by God or gods: from then on, humans were to be literally left to their own devices, also when it came to containing their own aggressiveness. The differences between the sacred and the profane became blurred, leading to what Girard terms a state of "undifferentation"—a confusion of social roles and an instability of cultural models and institutions. One of the crucial questions modernity faced was what to do with the cosmological vacuum left by God and how to cope with the effects of desacralisation. As the critic Peter Conrad observes, "among the many new claimants to divinity was man,"[9] though even at the outset his position proved strikingly precarious:

> Deicide may have been the nineteenth century's loftiest feat, but the victory was equivocal. Man enjoyed the favour of his creator, who singled him out from the animals, by conferring the gifts of reason and speech on him. Destroying our own begetter, had we not diminished ourselves?[10]

In the Girardian model, the erasure of differences is always potentially detrimental; the problem is that it has quite irrevocably become modernity's hallmark. Apart from confusing sacredness and profanity, the epoch of modernism was marked by a

---

9   Peter Conrad, *Modern Times, Modern Places: How Life and Art Were Transformed in a Century of Revolution, Innovation, and Radical Change*, (London: Thames and Hudson, 1998), 19.

10   Conrad, *Modern Times*, 23.

general trend towards the levelling of all distinctions. Many crowning achievements of modern Western civilisation, while no doubt introduced with a benevolent intent, had a devastating effect on cultural integrity. The consolidation of democracy and the free market economy, the increase in social equality, the widening of the franchise, the spread of feminism and the rise of the New Woman jolted people out of their domesticated timidity. The experience of living in a mass society, where everybody has more or less uniform needs and feels entitled to their satisfaction, enhanced the spirit of rivalry and gave the impetus for building tensions between human beings each desiring the same thing. The drive for self-realisation and perpetual expansion, manifest on various levels—among individuals, social classes, nation states—created a volatile atmosphere of awakened aspirations and conflicting desires.

A complex combination of these and other factors quite unexpectedly transformed the modern world from a civilised place, full of promise, into a competitive jungle. Discourses of violence began to flourish, and the attitude of dissent seemed curiously suited to the modern frame of mind. Calls for extreme action came from various directions: ideologues like Nietzsche spoke of a "great disengagement" from the past, Marxists were worked up by dreams of revolution, social Darwinists professed struggle to be man's most natural state, pioneers of psychoanalysis wished to free the instincts repressed by the civilising process. Social moods also became radicalised, as those who felt they had been suffering repression chose to stand up for their rights more assertively. Various subversive political movements, such as for example anarchism, were gaining popularity all over Europe; feminists became more violent in their opposition to male dominance; representatives of persecuted nations set up conspiratorial organisations, often of a militant character. Terrorism had already been well established as a method of achieving political ends: dynamite outrages, assassinations of politicians and even attacks on civilians—these were the threats that the European public was quite familiar with. On an international scale, the potential for violence was perceptible in the militarist and imperialist ambitions of the major political powers.

"You say it is the good cause that hallows even war? I tell you: it is the good war that hallows any cause."[11]—ran the perverted message of Nietzsche's Zarathustra. Written in 1891, his words needed only two decades to take root in the minds and hearts of many Europeans. As the signs of sacrificial crisis were intensifying, people began longing for some restorative, cathartic violence which could alter their predicament. The prospect of war, horrific as it may seem when assessed with the benefit of hindsight, was not altogether unwelcome at the beginning of the twentieth

---

11   Friedrich Nietzsche, *Thus Spoke Zarathustra*, Cambridge Texts in the History of Philosophy, Robert Pippin *et al*, eds. (Cambridge: Cambridge University Press, 2006), 33.

century. Historians and social critics often note that despite the idyllic picture of the pre-war decades preserved in the popular imagination,[12] the outbreak of hostilities in 1914 did not take anyone by surprise. Years before the conflict materialised, it had been talked and written about, rehearsed in creative activity and ideological rhetoric. Belligerent spirit was detectable in political pamphlets and treatises, such as Georges Sorel's *Reflections on Violence* (1908) or Friedrich von Bernhardi's *Germany and the Next War* (1912). The artistic circles also experienced contagion with an exalted state of militant readiness: painters, writers, critics and avant-garde performers indulged in innumerable struggles for cultural capital. Violence and aggressiveness were intertwined with new, revolutionary aesthetics propagated by the daringly modern movements, such as Futurism, Dadaism, Fauvism or Vorticism. The more cautious and catastrophically-minded writers and artists fed their audiences with images of explosions, mass graves and scarred landscapes, thus domesticating the demons of the not so distant future.

When the long awaited total war finally broke out, it led, after a brief moment of belligerent enthusiasm, to wholesale disenchantment. Rather than put modern minds at peace, it exacerbated the widespread sense of crisis and confirmed the inadequacy of past cultural models and institutions. Despite the fact that a whole generation of Europe's youth was ravaged on the battlefields, their sacrifice failed to have a cathartic effect. The atrocities of the war proved too great to earn the sanction of "rightful" violence; instead, doubt was cast on the idea of laying down one's life in the service of ideals. Massive collisions of millions of men in combat literally brought home horror and pain: nearly every family was forced to confront the consequences of modern violence. The war's political and economic impact was equally disastrous: it produced turmoil on the world markets and sowed the seeds of revolution, totalitarianism, fascism and state socialism in Europe. In the long run, far from being "the War to end all wars," the upheaval of 1914-1918 was a prelude to another cataclysmic convulsion, awaiting the Western world at the nearest turn of history.

---

12   The simplistic view of the decades preceding the First World War as "an age of innocence" has been challenged, among others, by Paul Fussel in *The Great War and Modern Memory* (Oxford: Oxford University Press, 1975) and by Samuel Hynes in *A War Imagined* (London: Pimlico, 1992). As many historians point out, the pre-war period was one of confrontation, tension and transition, and the talk of violence was more frequent than is usually assumed. In *The Missing of the Somme,* Geoff Dyer thus describes the pre-war Edwardian Britain: "Things were, of course, less settled than the habitual view of pre-August 1914 tempts us to believe. For many contemporary observers the war tainted the past, revealing and making explicit a violence that had been latent in the preceding peace. Eighty years on, this sense of crouched and gathering violence has been all but totally filtered out of our perception of the prewar period. Militant suffragettes, class unrest, strikes, Ireland teetering on the brink of civil war — all are shaded and softened by the long, elegiaic shadows cast by the war." Geoff Dyer, *The Missing of the Somme*, (London: Hamish Hamilton, 1994), 6.

The Secret Agent, Tarr and *Women in Love*

The present study attends to the trope of violence in three selected texts of early modernist fiction by placing them against the background of the historical and cultural whirl in which Western societies were caught up at the beginning of the twentieth century. The basis for such an exploration is the assumption that representation is grounded in historicity. As has been suggested so far, one way to explain the abundance of images of violence in modernist creations is to see them as a response to the specific state of crisis and an attempt to anticipate its potential ramifications. This imaginative exercise turns literature into a site of negotiation, projection and displacement of anxieties—a symbolic space where, it is hoped, that which is disturbing can be contained and made sense of.[13]

Among the vast body of British early modernist writings which thus address the confusions of their epoch, three novels suggest themselves as particularly suitable for consideration: Joseph Conrad's *The Secret Agent* (1907), Wyndham Lewis's *Tarr* (1918) and D.H. Lawrence's *Women in Love* (1920). Each of them investigates violence, understood as the abuse of physical force with the intention of causing harm to others. The phenomenon is not only registered and described in the three texts, but also explored from a number of perspectives, in connection with issues such as rationality, gender, legality, power and civilisation. This many-sidedness of treatment testifies to the centrality of the problem of violence to early twentieth-century culture, and indicates the multiple directions in which modern discourses on violence were progressing.

All three novels enter the debate over the nature and function of human aggression in ways that reflect the changing self-image of the epoch affected by the multiple threats of historical conflicts, revolutions and terrorist outrages. Each text comes from a different moment of the early modernist period and registers a different stage of the developing crisis; collectively, they span the time from the turn of the twentieth century to the end of the First World War. *The Secret Agent*, first serialized in 1906 and published in book form a year later, was inspired by the mysterious Greenwich bombing of 1894. Set in the late nineteenth century, it addresses anxieties related to political extremism, imperialism, and social unrest. The novel's central symbol is a bomb, which conveys a sense of violence as a potentiality, threatening to materialise unexpectedly and with great force. *Tarr*, written between 1907 and 1915, anticipates the

---

13   That this agenda is quite impossible to realise is another matter. As Arthur Redding observes, modernist attempts at "managing" the unsettling historical, social and political impulses must inevitably be frustrated. In confrontations with violence, the search for order and control is futile. See: Arthur Redding, *Raids on Human Consciousness,* (Columbia: University of South Carolina Press, 1998), 73, 118.

outbreak of international hostilities as it focuses on the intensifying masculine rivalry in the expatriate community of pre-war Paris. The book's controlling image is that of contagion, also in the sense of contamination by violence, spreading like an infectious disease from one character to the next. Finally, *Women in Love,* published in 1920, but taking shape during the most devastating years of World War I, between 1915 and 1917, portrays violence as an element of everyday life. Although the novel's temporal setting is indeterminate, Lawrence's representation of human aggression definitely has a wartime bleakness to it. The images of dissolution and corruption which pervade the book communicate a thoroughly pessimistic message that civilization is at an end and that people have sunk to the level of insensitive beasts.

It is a common feature of the three texts that they connect the intensification of aggression to the destructive trends of modern society. All picture the Western world as a hostile and alienating place, where community ties have been loosened and relationships become a struggle between dominance and humiliation. Driven by the logic of the capitalist economy, individuals devote all their energies to the ruthless pursuit of money, possession and power. It is in this context that the degradation of personality becomes more likely, and violence is allowed to germinate and then spread.

Mimetic Rivalries and Contagion of Violence

In analyses of specific instances of violence dramatised in the three novels, this study will apply the methodological apparatus provided by René Girard in his numerous works of anthropological theory, such as *Violence and the Sacred, The Scapegoat, Deceit, Desire and the Novel, Things Hidden Since the Foundation of the World, "To Double Business Bound": essays on Literature, Mimesis and Anthropology.* Apart from the notions of "sacrifice" and "sacrificial crisis," crucial to Girard's project is the idea of imitative rivalry, mimetic triangles, as well as the concept of violence as contamination.

According to Girard, all human conflicts are rooted in acquisitive mimesis—the fact that our desires are never autonomous but learnt from others by way of imitation. Rivalry results from a convergence of aspirations between people who are drawn towards the same object; if for some reason the object cannot be equally available to the competing parties, they become locked in a triangular relationship where mimesis and difference are experienced together in tension. Frustrated rivals turn into "monstrous doubles," forever trying to surpass, but ending up mirroring, each other.[14] Escalation of such reciprocity creates the risk of violence which itself is reciprocal and contagious. The passion aroused by an act of hostility can only be quelled by a similar act and if

---

14   René Girard, *Violence and the Sacred,* Trans. Patrick Gregory, (London: The Athlone Press, 1988), 161. Elements of Girard's theoretical model are further discussed in Chapter III.

a person who has been attacked cannot rise above the desire for vengeance, he will replicate the behaviour of the aggressor. Additionally, an exchange of violent gestures usually attracts the interest of those who find themselves near to mimetic rivals and who become involved in the conflict by supporting one of the sides.[15] In this way, violence can spread like a contagious disease, drawing more and more people into the maelstrom of destructive reciprocity.

Once violence has erupted, the situation can easily get out of control, because, as Burton L. Mack observes, humans have no instinctual protection against intraspecific aggression.[16] They will not stop short of manslaughter, and their weapons enable them to fight to the kill. The mimetic process of violent escalation can only be brought to a halt by culturally imposed means, that is through the victimage mechanism and the social institutions which stem from it. At the most basic level, conflicts are resolved by scapegaoating some "surrogate victim" against whom rivals, or whole communities, can unite. "Unanimity minus one" is a model which allows for a displacement of rage: it nullifies the discomfort of sameness, for the warring sides must now define themselves in opposition to the scapegoat. New, "sacred" rules of relating are established and supported by the development of mythology whose function is to ensure the preservation of peace. Myths help to conceal the arbitrariness of the choice of the victim, as well as the fact that the victim is innocently persecuted.

As has been mentioned before, it is this last, mythic aspect of violence that modern Western society has difficulty with. The old mechanisms of mimetic rivalry, reciprocal abuse and victimisation continue to operate, but their justification is growing more and more problematic. On the one hand, the "sacredness" of cultural arrangements is put in doubt, but on the other, people are not yet prepared to function without the mythic vision. This explains why moments when societies attempt to see through their myths and begin to talk about responsibility and justice are so extremely precarious: it is then that the temptation to revert to the old models and to the logic of clear-cut good-and-bad polarities is the highest. In Girard's own words,

> Men cannot confront the naked truth of their own violence without the risk of abandoning themselves to it entirely. They have never had a very clear idea of this violence, and it is possible that the survival of all human societies of the past was dependent on this fundamental lack of understanding.[17]

---

15   Girard, *Violence and the Sacred*, 14-15, 28.

16   Burton L. Mack, Introduction to *Violent Origins: Walter Burkert, René Girard and Jonathan Z. Smith on Ritual Killing and Cultural Formation*, Robert Hamerton-Kelly, ed., (Stanford: Stanford University Press, 1987), 8.

17   Girard, *Violence and the Sacred*, 82.

The early twentieth century must have been a moment of such dicing with danger, given the mass slaughter of the Great War and other dramatic events that followed. It therefore seems a valid task for literary criticism to try to detect traces of the phenomena described by Girard in the creative output of modernist writers. If literature registers cultural tensions, then it should also register any attempts at meddling with the culture's mythical foundations. The confusion resulting from the questioning of "sacred" solutions, the glimpses of human self-knowledge, the allure of the traditional victimisation dynamic—all these are likely to be present in modernist texts.

The Violence Mythos of Modernism

While this study depends for its methodological anchors on the works of Girard, a discussion of the modernist contribution to the general discourse of violence would be incomplete without a reference to Barbara Whitmer's concept of "the violence mythos." In her book-length meditation on the nature and significance of violence in human society, she provides a useful framework for cultural and disciplinary analyses of the subject:

> *The violence mythos* is a collection of beliefs, attitudes, behaviours, and social expectations about violence in Western culture. Violence is defined as injurious or destructive discourse or action of one person or group toward another. The violence mythos includes the war hero myth, the victimizer/victim dynamic of exploitation, the theory of innate violence, the myth of competitive individualism, the mind/body dualism, the myth of male aggression and the subordination of women, the myth of the superiority of rationality over emotion, the myth of the elite human species, and the development of technology in a tradition of destructive instrumentalism.[18]

Applying Whitmer's definition to the analysis of *The Secret Agent*, *Tarr*, and *Women in Love*, this study will attempt to establish what elements of the Western violence mythos these novels propagate. As far as possible, it will also try to locate Conrad's, Lewis's and Lawrence's creations in relation to the prevalent cultural attitudes of their time.

Of course, any extensive analysis of such issues exceeds the scope of the present study, so the commentary upon the late nineteenth- and early twentieth-century stance on violence must necessarily be limited to a summary form. In general, it can be stated that a majority of the then popular discourses construed aggressiveness as innate to human species and therefore impossible to eradicate completely. As the doctrine of social Darwinism made clear, humans want to wage war against each other, for such is their biological makeup. The assumption of "a death instinct" that came with the rise

---

18   Whitmer, *The Violence Mythos*, 1.

of psychoanalysis did not, essentially, change this perspective: the dynamic of violence appeared to be a part of a natural order. The purpose of culture, posited in opposition to nature, was to restrain violence under the rubric of civilisational control. In other words, external community structures were seen as necessary to protect humans against themselves, in the name of cultural survival. A system of civilised institutions was then able to legitimate, rationalise, and use violence against aggressive individuals as a means of social control. As Girard would put it, institutional, or state, violence was recognised as sacred, or benevolent, whereas some kinds of individual violence (the more brutal acts, such as killing or mutilation of others) were classed as malevolent, aberrant, or profane.

The idea of putting a curb of civilisational control over nature remained in agreement with the rational, industrial and scientific vision which saw the world in terms of a binary opposition between spirit and matter. The emphasis on the natural sciences promoted an understanding of the material world as a machine, operating in accordance with a predictable, unchanging set of rules. All this was accompanied by the belief in the elite status of the human species: man, occupying the top position in the natural hierarchy, was supposed to make good use of his gift of reason and ensure order in the world of which he was master. With the cultural transition to modernism, however, this complacent view of reality had to undergo a thorough revision: the developing distrust of civilisation, the collapse of binary epistemological models, the corruption of "sacred" notions such as "honour," "patriotism," and "glory" as a result of the experience of the first total war called into question the validity of the Western violence mythos.

Review of Critical Approaches to Violence and Modernism

Despite the turn to history and culture in literary criticism, the modernist novel's engagement with violence has not been explored too often. Apart from the question of World War I, which has always attracted critical attention, there has been little research on representations of violence as such, or on their ideological content. In the past, analysts of modernist fiction shunned approaching the subject of violence in isolation, perhaps obeying the taboo which to some degree still surrounds it,[19] or simply seeing the issue as unworthy of academic examination. Borrowing a phrase from Conrad, one might say that aggression and brutality were perceived as things that "do not stand much looking into" (*SA* 162). They were made more manageable when treated as part and parcel of some larger problem (e.g. war)—then, on the one hand, their presence appeared more natural and, on the other, they could be easily marginalised, or just mentioned in passing. The

---

19   As various cultural critics have pointed out, Western culture condemns violence as evil, but pays little attention to understanding its origins, or to studying the prevalent discourses of human aggression.

situation began to change about a decade ago, when the question of violence was brought into focus of the Western world as a result of the terrorist attacks in the US and Europe.

A number of publications from recent years can be listed as notable attempts at filling the critical gap in the study of violence in modernist fiction. Perhaps the most important among them is William A. Johnsen's *Violence and Modernism: Ibsen, Joyce, Woolf* (2002), which analyses the works of three canonical figures in the light of René Girard's and Northrop Frye's investigations of the mythical base of modern society. Johnsen's interest is in how Ibsen, Joyce and Woolf question the scapegoating mechanisms present in Western culture and propose "a redefinion of the modern away from mimetic rivalry and violence, towards a tradition of peaceful identity and reciprocity."[20] This is a very positive reading of the modernist achievement and the literary giants Johnsen is concerned with do indeed offer a critique of human aggressiveness in a manner consistent with that of Girard. However, unlike the writers discussed in the present study, Ibsen, Joyce and Woolf rarely attempt direct depictions of violence, and if they do so, their narration is marked with detachment, preventing identification with perpetrators of violent acts.

Two publications by the author quoted at the beginning of this chapter, Terry Eagleton, also draw attention to a return of myth in modern times and see violence, trauma and victimisation as important components of Western cultural production. *Sweet Violence* (2003), discussing the idea of the tragic, and its follow-up, *Holy Terror* (2005) are broad in scope and content, and will no doubt serve as inspiration for more focused academic undertakings in the future. In the latter work, Eagleton examines the concept of terror in numerous literary sources, including *The Secret Agent* and *Women in Love.*

Among the slightly earlier critical contributions, Arthur F. Redding's *Raids on Human Consciousness: Writing, Anarchism and Violence* (1998) deserves a mention as an interesting meditation on the connection between violence and literature. While the timespan of Redding's study includes modern and post-modern culture, two sections of his book are devoted to the analysis of modernist texts. As he observes quite rightly, we should remember that it was not only the violence of the First World War that shaped modernist creations, but also "the dynamite talk" linked to the idea of anarchism. According to Redding,

> [o]ne fracture crisscrossing the epistemic fault line of aesthetic modernism is the person of the anarchist, who challenges the political engines of the will to knowledge and forces confrontations. Before fantasies of violence, knowledge is compelled to retreat. Loosely, modernism might be called the formal version of the "textualization" of violence.[21]

---

20   William A. Johnsen, *Violence and Modernism: Ibsen, Joyce, Woolf,* (Gainesville: University Press of Florida, 2002), xiii.

21   Redding, *Raids on Human Consciousness*, 118.

Redding's observation remains in close proximity to the thesis of David Weir, the author of *Anarchy and Culture: The Aesthetic Politics of Modernism* (1997), who also isolates the figure of the anarchist, or even the terrorist, as crucial to modernist enterprise. The insights offered by Weir and Redding are compelling but at the same problematic, because they overemphasize the influence of just one type of violent ideology. The exact understanding of the word "anarchism" is in itself a source of confusion: both critics seem to conflate anarchism and terrorism a little too easily, concentrating mainly on the militant aspect of what was a complex and multi-faceted cultural and political phenomenon.[22]

Another publication concerned with modern literature in general but quite sensitive to its preoccupation with violence is Peter Conrad's *Modern Times, Modern Places: How Life and Art Were Transformed in a Century of Revolution, Innovation, and Radical Change* (1998). Conrad surveys the cultural production of the twentieth century, observing how modernity celebrates aggression and destruction. In an attempt to capture the mood of the pre-war period, he writes:

> Modernity, which suddenly increased velocity in all areas of human experience, resembled a rollercoaster: a voluntary ride, thrilling, because it jested with disaster. The dangers were optional, not predestined. They derived, in a society which had rejected traditional guidance about who we are, from the revelation that identity is tenuous, as mutable as the earth which is forever being eruptively transformed.[23]

Conrad is also one of the critics who do not see modernism's interest in violence solely in terms of the impact of World War I, but paints a larger picture, drawing attention to the twentieth-century early years, extremely tense socially and politically, and full of pent-up negative energy.

Of course, the shadow that the Great War cast on modernism should by no means be disregarded, and there exist numerous critical works, many already considered classics, which do justice to this question in a comprehensive way. Among them, Samuel Hynes's *A War Imagined* (1992) and Modris Ekstein's *Rites of Spring: The Great War and the Birth of the Modern Age* (1989) are perhaps the most notable. Both texts stress the fact that the war was a difficult exercise in imagination for every thoughtful person living in its wake. Artistic and literary responses to it entailed a redefinition of attitudes to violence, sacrifice, suffering and loss, so in terms of creative expression the war paved the way for an entirely new era. Other

---

22   I discuss this question in greater detail in the article „Bunt przeciw *arche*? Elementy myśli anarchistycznej w brytyjskim modernizmie," published in: Krystyna Stamirowska, ed., *Historia, fikcja, (auto)biografia w powieści brytyjskiej XX wieku,* (Kraków: Universitas, 2006), 91-113.

23   Conrad, *Modern Times,* 16.

attempts to situate the achievement of literary modernism in relation to the Great War include Trudi Tate, *Modernism, History and the First World War* (1998), and Allyson Booth, *Postcards from the Trenches: Negotiating the Space between Modernism and the First World War* (1996), however both texts are less concerned with modernist representations of violence than with the boundaries between modernism and war writing.

As regards criticism of Conrad, Lewis and Lawrence, no separate studies have been published to date that would concern themselves specifically with any of the three writers' interest in violence. As was the case with the general surveys of modernism, also with respect to particular authors and texts, violence tends to be analysed within wider contexts, and not as a separate issue.

Of the three writers discussed in the present thesis, Conrad has probably received the best critical coverage with regard to his meditations on human depravity. There exist numerous publications exploring the ethical content of his work, his social critique and perspectives on history. One of the studies which touch upon Conrad's interest in the problem of violence is Allan Hunter's *Joseph Conrad and the Ethics of Darwinism* (1983). It tackles Conrad's work in the light of post-Darwinian challenge, debates of cultural progression and retrogression, as well as turn-of-the-century discourses of criminology and eugenics. Similar issues have also been discussed by John W. Griffith in *Joseph Conrad and the Anthropological Dilemma: A Bewildered Traveller* (1995). Both Hunter's and Griffith's studies portray Conrad as an anthropologically conscious figure, well versed in theories of culture and civilisation and not afraid to challenge the various notions and opinions prevalent in his time. For anyone researching violence in Conrad's texts, these two critical works are a necessary read, for although neither of them attempts any direct treatment of the issue, they nevertheless supply extensive background knowledge of Victorian and Edwardian anthropology.

When it comes to critical readings of the *The Secret Agent* itself, the novel has recently enjoyed a revival of academic interest, focusing mainly on the subjects of anarchism and—in the aftermath of the 2001 September 11 attacks—also terrorism. The latter has been explored most compellingly by Alex Houen in *Terrorism and Modern Literature: From Joseph Conrad to Ciaran Carson* (2002). In his chapter on Conrad, Houen discusses the novel's engagement with terrorism in the light of entropic theories[24] and the Second Law of Thermodynamics; he also places *The Secret Agent* in relation to "the legacy of terrorism that Britain inherited at the beginning of the twentieth century."[25]

---

24   This idea was first explored by Brian Spittles, who in his *Joseph Conrad: Text and Context* notes the importance of the entropic theory to Conrad's work. See: "The Entropic Labyrinth," in: Brian Spittles, *Joseph Conrad: Text and Context,* (London: Macmillan, 1992), 139-159.

25   Alex Houen, *Terrorism in Modern Literature: From Joseph Conrad to Ciaran Carson,* (Oxford: Oxford University Press, 2002), 21.

As regards the question of anarchism in Conrad, it has been studied from every possible perspective, beginning with the historical context of the Greenwich bomb outrage (Vincent Sherry, David Mulry), through the psychology of the anarchist characters (Carol Vanderveer Hamilton, Helen Funk Rieselbach, Martin Ray), down to the anarchist theories of language (Paul Hollywood). Some of these analyses include discussions of violence, but they are always secondary to the main argument.

Another interesting direction in which studies of *The Secret Agent* have recently evolved is the search for Gothic and *noir* elements, as well as Dostoevskian influences in the text. This trend locates Conrad's work within a wider literary tradition, either that of the nineteenth (Gothic), or the twentieth century (*noir*). One of the most insightful interpretations of this kind has been offered by Lee Horsley, who in her book *The Noir Thriller* (2001), sees *The Secret Agent* as an early example of *noir* fiction. Modernist pessimism, Horsley argues, played a significant role in establishing the hallmarks of *noir* as it produced works permeated with an atmosphere of doom and peopled with guilty, vulnerable characters, struggling to make sense of the disturbing realities around them. Oppressive settings, gloomy imagery, the unstable identities of the protagonists, fate as an unrelenting force rendering all human efforts futile—all this instils in modernist literature a *noir* tone; a quality which modernist techniques such as the use of ironic distance, subjective narration, multiplicity of viewpoints and non-linear plot are particularly well suited to bring out.

Many characteristics of *The Secret Agent* justify Horsley's observation: the novel's protagonists find themselves in an alienating universe where the traditional order of things is unsettled and where no one can be trusted; the plot turns on misconceptions and contradictions; the emphasis falls on the irrational and the inexplicable; there is an air of fatality about the characters' actions, and apprehension of an impending disaster. The *noir* themes and imagery are further reinforced by the stylistic qualities of the text, especially the dispassionate narrative voice which appears to be completely discrepant with the horrors it recounts. Oscillating between farce and tragedy, *The Secret Agent* evokes a Kafkaesque atmosphere of absurdity in which the protagonists—pathetically self-deluded, incapable of communicating with others and blind to the real nature of events they are a part of—remain trapped.

In comparison to the amount of critical attention devoted to Conrad, Wyndham Lewis has suffered considerable neglect, despite his high profile presence on the modernist scene and his double genius as painter and writer. Self-styled as "the Enemy," he remains the hard man of British modernism, rarely analysed and frequently misread. For years, he has been branded with the label of "fascist," partly as a result of the political views he espoused in the years prior to World War II, and partly due to the popularity of Fredric Jameson's critical study *Fables of Aggression: Wyndham Lewis, the Modernist as Fascist,* which, published in 1979, greatly influenced the general tenor of Lewis criticism.[26] It has been only recently—for about a decade and a half—that a growing number of critics have attempted to look beyond the received view of Lewis, based largely on the biographical appeal and not on consideration of his work.

Criticism of Lewis's literary work is still relatively scarce, as he is mostly studied as both a painter and a writer. The novel *Tarr* has never been made the subject of a separate critical volume. With the notable exceptions of Paul Edwards, Michael Levenson, Paul Peppis, Andrzej Gąsiorek, Jeffrey Meyers and Toby Foshay, few critics have devoted more than a sub-chapter of a book to *Tarr*'s analysis. This is rather regrettable, considering how highly *Tarr* was thought of upon its publication: Ezra Pound, T.S. Eliot and Rebecca West all hailed it as a book initiating a new type of writing. As Lewis himself observes in his autobiography of 1937, in the early years of World War I, *Tarr* "looked queer," because "it did not conform to the traditional wave-length of the English Novel."[27]

Despite the limited amount of critical work on Lewis available, he seems to be often placed in the contexts of violence and aggression. Some of these readings are obviously disfiguring and reflective of what Alan Munton diagnoses as the popular tendency to "impute noxiousness" to Lewis because of his "Enemy" status[28]; others are valuable attempts to relate Lewis's work to the historical reality which defined its creation. Among the latter, *Wyndham Lewis and the Art of Modern War*, edited by David Peters Corbett, is probably the most wide-ranging in its exploration of violence as one of the central themes of Lewis's *oeuvre*. A collective work of renowned Wyndham Lewis scholars (Paul Edwards, Alan Munton, Tom Normand, David A. Wragg, among others), it offers a reassessment of Lewis as a commentator on his own times and places him at the centre of the modernist response to a foundational aspect of twentieth-century culture. The contributors to the volume examine Lewis's painting, writing, politics and aesthetics in connection with his experience of the First and Second World Wars, as well as to the Cold War. Obviously, the broad scope of the

---

26 The problem with Jameson's highly influential study of Lewis is that it has an unfortunate title (despite implications of fascism and violence, Jameson's argument is more subtle than his title suggests) and that it was written by a critic and theorist whose authority few scholars dare to question. Jameson proposes to construct a "model" of the psyche of Lewis's texts, the so-called "libidinal apparatus," registering cultural and political forces beyond his control. Such reading ignores the historical circumstances of Lewis's career and tries to explain the writer's interest in right wing ideas by concentrating on his psychological difficulty. See: Fredric Jameson, *Fables of Aggression: Wyndham Lewis, the Modernist as Fascist*, (Berkeley: University of California Press, 1979).

27 Wyndham Lewis, *Blasting and Bombardiering* (1937), (London: John Calder, 1982), 88-89.

28 In his articles in *Wyndham Lewis Annual*, Alan Munton has been regularly campaigning against the critical habit of speaking ill of Lewis. As he observes, "Lewis is so widely reviled that almost any claim about him, or his work, can be made. That he, or his work, is violent, fascist, mysogynist and pathologically insane has become, not the end-point of argument, but the point of departure." See: Alan Munton, "'Imputing Noxiousness': Aggression and Mutilation in Recent Lewis Criticism," *Wyndham Lewis Annual*, (Vol.IV, 1997), 5.

publication is also its disadvantage: striving to give an overall picture, it leaves out the detail necessary for the full appreciation of Lewis's achievement.

Among the critical accounts which make a connection between Lewis and violence there is the already mentioned Alex Houen's *Terrorism and Modern Literature* (2002). In the chapter entitled "Wyndham Lewis: Literary Strikes and Allegorical Assaults" Houen posits English Vorticism against Italian Futurism, explores the historical circumstances of the publication of Lewis's magazine *Blast*, the play *Enemy of the Stars* and the short story *Cantleman's Spring Mate.* Discussing Lewis's avant-garde responses to Syndicalism and the militant Suffragette movement, Houen portrays Lewis as a literary terrorist, espousing aesthetics of violence. In a sense, then, despite the attempt to locate Lewis's work in a specific moment in history, Houen subscribes to the routine critical practice of imputing violent intention to Lewis. If the later Lewis is stereotyped as fascist, the earlier Lewis tends to be stereotyped as a terrorist just on account of using militant language in his avant-garde publications.

As regards critical discussions of *Tarr,* the question of violence represented in the novel does not attract too much attention. The critic who seems most sensitive to this issue is Dennis Brown; sadly, in his book entitled *Intertextual Dynamics within the Literary Group—Joyce, Lewis, Pound and Eliot: The Men of 1914* (1990) he spares only four pages for *Tarr's* analysis. Other readings of *Tarr* include: Paul Peppis's brilliant examination of Lewis's national stereotypes, Alistair Davies's much contested discussion of *Tarr* as a Nietzschean novel, and David Trotter's controversial diagnosis of *Tarr* as a paranoid narrative with elements of schizophrenia.

Perhaps the most compelling interpretation of Lewis's novel is the one proposed by Michael Levenson in *Modernism and the Fate of Individuality* (1991). Levenson claims the modernist novelty of *Tarr* lies in the fact that Lewis obliterates the boundaries of identity and that the character features are "transitive," that is, can pass freely from one protagonist to the next:

> Character [in *Tarr*] is not a unique configuration of traits, nor a bounded essence; it is a *condition* that can pass beyond the usual boundaries of subjectivity, branding, tainting, contaminating others. Much of the struggle between individuals takes the form of a struggle to impose one character upon another.[29]

Levenson's argument is taken as a point of departure for the chapter on *Tarr* in the present study, which investigates violence as a form of contagion and focuses on how aggression spreads among the novel's masculine characters by way of Girardian mirroring.

---

29   Michael Levenson, *Modernism and the Fate of Individuality*, (Cambridge: Cambridge University Press, 1991), 134.

The third modernist figure that is the subject of this analysis, D.H. Lawrence, is almost as well explored critically as Conrad. Moreover, because *Women in Love* is often seen as Lawrence's best work, most analysts feel obliged to include it in their research, which results in a proliferation of interpretations. As Melvyn Bragg observes, interest in the novel has come in waves: "[*Women in Love*] has gone in and out of fashion and will again slide evasively through that fool's gold of merely fashionable opinion."[30] For the last decade, Lawrence criticism in general has enjoyed a revival: his work is currently being reconsidered within an intriguing set of new contexts, and from new theoretical perspectives. It is therefore quite surprising that a separate study of the trope of violence in Lawrence's work has not yet appeared, despite the fact that he seems one of the most obvious candidates for this kind of analysis.

Among the most interesting explorations of Lawrence's achievement, there is, for example, Andrew Harrison's *D.H. Lawrence and Italian Futurism: A Study of Influence* (2003). It captures the similarities between the Lawrencean and Futurist attitudes to modernity, at the same time recognising the areas where Lawrence diverges from the Futurist perpective. Harrison shows awareness of the inherent discrepancy between the Futurist exaltation of the machine and Lawrence's assertion of the natural man; in the chapter on *Women in Love* this aspect of Lawrence's Futurist adventure comes very clearly into focus. With regard to the problem of violence, Harrison notes that the tendency which informs much of Lawrence's early work—to invest outbursts of aggression with cathartic value—is given a reconsideration in the wake of the Great War.

The impact of the First World War on Lawrence's creative output has been also investigated by Helen Wussow. *The Nightmare of History: the Fiction of Virginia Woolf and D.H. Lawrence* (1998) is a valuable comparative study of two modernist figures who at first sight may appear strange bedfellows. Covering almost the entire fictional *oeuvres* of the two writers, Wussow shows how Lawrence's and Woolf's responses to history complement one another. Considerable attention is also devoted to the way in which both modernists write conflict into their fictions, but the ambitious scope of Wussow's project prevents her from analysing representations of violence in very great detail.

Yet another study which attempts to historicise Lawrence, at the same time putting his work in a philosophical perspective, is Simon Casey's *Naked Liberty and the World of Desire: Elements of Anarchism in the Work of D.H. Lawrence* (2003). Tracing Lawrence's engagement with libertarian philosophy, Casey takes Lawrence criticism off the beaten track: the insights he offers challenge many of the traditional interpretations of Lawrence's fiction. For example, a re-reading of the "murderer and

---

30   Melvyn Bragg, Introduction to the Cambridge Edition of D.H. Lawrence's *Women in Love*, (London: Grafton Books, 1988), vii.

murderee" theory in *Women in Love* emphasises an anarchist viewpoint on Birkin's part and an optimistic belief that human nature is social in its essence. Casey's work reveals the utopian and idealistic side of Lawrence, and is therefore useful to anyone who researches violence, in that it may counterbalance some of the seemingly dark and gloomy conclusions drawn from Lawrence's texts.

As far as criticism of *Women in Love* is concerned, there have recently been so many innovative approaches to the novel that it would be futile to try to enumerate them. Among the most intriguing ones are: James Twitchell's examination of the male-female relationships in the novel in terms of the vampire myth, Jack F. Stewart's analysis of the Biblical motif of the fall, Kingsley Widmer's discussion of desire, or Wayne Templetone's exploration of the themes of estrangement and alienation. All of these critical readings quite naturally touch upon the subject of violence, but without attempting any decisive statements as to what message about human aggressivity Lawrence's text may be trying to communicate.

As this brief and, admittedly, selective overview of criticism has shown, there are still gaps to fill in the existing extensive body of research on the British modernism's three major presences. With regard to the question of violence, there is certainly a need for a shift of interpretative focus from the figures of the writers themselves (especially in the case of Lewis and Lawrence) to the actual content of their works. Modernist studies would also benefit from an intensification of research devoted to the period preceding the 1922 *annus mirabilis*, especially to the time before the Great War. While the War's impact on modernist engagement with violence cannot be questioned, investigating other influences still seems a tempting critical task. This study, far too modest in scope to seriously undertake any of the above challenges, is meant to take a small step in the new direction.

CHAPTER II

Ticking Towards Disaster—Violence as "The Enemy Within" in Conrad's *The Secret Agent*

In England the ground appears solid and the structure of State firm, to a superficial observer. But if he lay his ear to the ground . . . and if he examine the walls closer, he will see that underneath the varnish and gold plating, dangerous cracks extend from top to bottom.

Max Nordau, *The Conventional Lies of Our Civilisation*

"An explosion is the most lasting thing in the universe. It leaves disorder, remembrance, room to move, a clear space,"[31] declares Conrad in one of his letters. At the turn of the twentieth century, when these words were written, explosions had a certain allure: their energy and potential for energising appealed to the human need for an instant change, a radical break with the past, a complete redefinition of reality. The new was to arrive with a cathartic big bang—a starting point for a transvaluation of all values that, according to the epoch's key philosopher, Nietzsche, could finally redeem the erring human race. History proved otherwise: blasts, detonations and other destructive outbursts quickly became modernity's gloomy emblems, though they were rarely followed by the positive developments they had initially promised. Conrad must have had a premonition of this when in 1907, while working on *The Secret Agent*, he made an explosion the main event of the plot and peopled his book with characters who carry inflammable ideas. Bombs exploding and waiting to explode, the old world ticking towards eruption, human beings like sticks of dynamite, on the verge of psychological detonation—these are the subjects that he tackles, expressing in this way the modernist sense of precariousness and instability.

---

31 Conrad to Garnett, 12 March, 1897, in: Joseph Conrad, *The Collected Letters of Joseph Conrad: Volume I, 1861-1897*, Frederick R. Karl, ed., (Cambridge: Cambridge University Press, 1983), 334.

Violence is thus central to Conrad's text and is distinctly bomb-like in nature. It operates by way of abrupt energetic discharges, sending shock waves through the lives of the main protagonists and shattering seemingly unshakeable relationships and arrangements. It also exists as a potentiality, ever-present in the novel's murky universe, where forces of chaos may at any moment rip apart the façade of familiarity and order. The "secret agent" of the title can be read as a metaphor for the annihilation principle endemic at all levels of human organisation, interaction and existence. Everything, from the structures of society at large, through family ties, down to an individual psyche, hides an enemy within, some explosive material awaiting ignition. The critic Con Coroneos observes that Conrad's writing is generally "disturbed by troubled interiors (hollow men, void mines, burst eardrums, windy idealisms, and rotting cargoes)"[32]; *The Secret Agent*—with bad energy caged in the most innocuous containers—seems to be yet another variation on the theme. The tension in the novel comes from the risk of a violent enucleation, an advertent or inadvertent release of some anomalous content which can never be brought under control again. After the novel's climactic blast occurs, chaos enters the scene: the chronology of the plot is disrupted, and the characters spend the remaining time trying to find out what happened and how to come to terms with it. Never represented directly, the actual explosion is only accessible to the reader through scraps of information coming from various sources. As Lee Horsley rightly points out, the task of piecing the puzzle together underscores the ultimate difficulty, or even impossibility, of "arriving at any secure knowledge by means of orderly inquiry."[33]

In the Author's Note Conrad confesses that his book was inspired by true events, namely the obscure detonation in Greenwich Park in February 1894 when a French anarchist was blown up by his own bomb. His intentions were never discovered, but clearly there must have been a failure of his plans, as he was the incident's only casualty and the nearby Greenwich Observatory—a possible target of the anarchist outrage— did not "show as much as the faintest crack" (*SA* xxix). Despite its negligible destructive effect, the blast caused considerable hysteria in the press and among the general public, who were suddenly forced to revise their view of London as a relatively safe place to live. Until then, militant anarchism had been considered a continental malaise and although Britain was a haven for subversive political refugees, it was assumed their activity would not go beyond inconclusive plotting. The only bombings that ever troubled Victorian London were linked to the Irish Home Rule movement and occurred almost a decade before, so the impression was that propaganda by the deed had exhausted itself as a

---

32   Con Coroneos, *Space, Conrad and Modernity*, (Oxford: Oxford University Press, 2002), 42.

33   Lee Horsley, *The Noir Thriller*, (London: Palgrave, 2001), 12.

means of nationalist struggle.[34] The explosion in Greenwich was a wake-up call, a signal of brewing trouble, made all the more sinister by the aura of secrecy surrounding it. As Conrad's authorial commentary suggests, the incident's most disturbing quality was inexplicability—the fact that it evaded rationalisation and could not be readily sanctioned by ideology or any other purpose:

> in a casual conservation about anarchists, or rather anarchist activities . . . we recalled the already old story of the attempt to blow up the Greenwich Observatory; a blood stained inanity of so fatuous a kind that it was impossible to fathom its origin by any reasonable or even unreasonable process of thought. For perverse unreason has its own logical processes. But that outrage could not be laid hold of mentally in any sort of way, so that one remained faced with a man blown to bits for nothing even most remotely resembling an idea, anarchistic or other (*SA* xxix).

Pondering upon the circumstances of the bizarre occurrence, Conrad apprehended its symbolic implications. The bomb in Greenwich was like a sudden intrusion of the chaotic and irrational into the hitherto orderly functioning of a modern metropolis. It served as a reminder that there is a flip-side to reality as we know it, a hidden realm beyond the grasp of our cognition, possibly harbouring a counter-culture. The blown up anarchist was a visitor from the underworld, a disclosed element of a secret narrative that had been going on subterraneanly, alongside the familiar current of the urban life. An unexpected manifestation of this repressed potential was to evoke fear and a sense of vulnerability, especially as it was not possible to unravel the rest of the anarchist story and assess the real extent of the threat. In a world which takes reason as its frame of reference that which is unfathomable is *ipso facto* dangerous and malevolent; uncharted territories are conceived as hearts of darkness. One of the greatest fears of the rational man is a loss of control, for understanding is a form of control, a way to rise triumphant over chaos and uncertainty. Thus, the Greenwich explosion frustrated the minds of Conrad's contemporaries and struck a deep chord with the writer, who probably saw in it a kind of existential epiphany, an event which epitomised the anxiety resulting from a confrontation with the unknowable.

Reflection on the outrage spawned a novel based on a constant dialectic between security and threat, suffused with a recognition that apparent normality is actually the antithesis of what it seems to be and that disaster must strike when and where it

---

34 For factual analyses of the Greenwich Park explosion, see: Norman Sherry, *Conrad's Western World*, (Cambridge: Cambridge University Press, 1971) and David Mulry, "Popular accounts of the Greenwich bombing and Conrad's *The Secret Agent*," *Rocky Mountain Review*, (Washington University Press: Fall 2000), 43-64.

is least expected. Every plan and every construct can be destroyed by an insidious saboteur: the "opulent luxury" of the London privileged classes may be imperilled by the "unhygienic proletariat" (*SA* 10), the crowd in the streets is bound to face the resentment of the misanthropic Professor, the Verlocs' marriage is doomed to failure because of mutual deception, Stevie's body is betrayed by its own awkwardness, and the desperate Winnie becomes cheated by a man whom she imagines to be her saviour. Lee Horsley, who classifies Conrad's text as an early example of the *noir* thriller, draws attention to the fact that it denies every possibility of trust by creating "a picture of a society in which everyone is a 'secret agent' and no one is to be taken at face value, in which no appearances actually correspond to realities and in which supposed order is revealed to be anarchy."[35]

One of the secret agents in this world of universal conspiracy is violence. It takes the form of unanticipated visitations from dark forces underlying manifest reality: that which is thought to have been repressed by the existing social organisation and the civilizing process suddenly leaps out and proves its potency. The novel's figures of dread—characters who plan or perpetrate violent deeds—act surreptitiously, exploiting the naivety or complacency of their unassuming victims. Sometimes they too are taken aback by their own proclivity for aggression, as is the case with Winnie who kills her husband in a fit of abandon and then cannot face the consequences of her action. Violence proves a mystery even to those who consciously bring it about: Vladimir, Verloc, and the Professor all have to acknowledge that no amount of strategic thinking can ensure the desired outcome—it is impossible to entertain a fantasy of control if one's activities are meant to usher in chaos. Associated with the threat of the unknown and unforeseen, violence functions in *The Secret Agent* as something which reason cannot contain, a kind of ultimate "otherness," forever impenetrable to the human mind, and therefore irreformable. Always latent in the individual and in society, it seems to be ticking like a bomb, the strength of which may only be assessed *post factum*, after an explosion takes place.

A dramatisation of the shadowy potential lurking behind our assumed condition is probably the most important aspect of Conrad's portrayal of violence. His novelistic imagination explores the possibility of the "dark side" taking over and civilisation yielding to the rule of chaos and savagery. Like many writers and thinkers of his cultural milieu, Conrad suspects that mankind's progress is being perpetually sabotaged by a drive towards death and destruction. An often quoted letter to Cunnighame Graham, of February 1898, plainly spells out his scepticism about the possibility of improving human nature:

---

35   Horsley, *The Noir Thriller,* 11.

Into the noblest cause men manage to put something of their baseness; and sometimes when I think of You here, quietly, you seem to me tragic with your courage, with your beliefs and your hopes. Every cause is tainted: and you reject this one, espouse that other one as if one were evil and the other good while the same evil you hate is in both, but disguised in different words. I am more in sympathy with you than words can express yet if I had a grain of belief left in me I would believe you misguided. You are misguided by the desire of the impossible—and I envy you. Alas! What you want to reform are not institutions—it is human nature. Your faith will never move that mountain. Not that I think mankind is intrinsically bad. It is only silly and cowardly. Now You know that in cowardice is every evil—especially that cruelty so characteristic of our civilisation. But without it mankind would vanish. No great matter truly. But will you persuade humanity to throw away the sword and the shield? Can you persuade even me—who writes these words in the fullness of an irresistible conviction? No. I belong to the wretched gang. We all belong to it. We are born initiated, and succeeding generations clutch the inheritance of fear and brutality without a thought, without a doubt, without compunction—in the name of God.[36]

It is not surprising that, as a believer in man's Hobbesean temperament, Conrad should be inclined towards gloomy, dystopian visions. As numerous critics have shown, the anxieties and preoccupations of *The Secret Agent* are inextricably bound up with late nineteenth- and early twentieth-century discourses of civilisational decline, entropic drift, Darwinist struggle, social disintegration, class and sex wars, and atavistic regression.[37] Violence features in all of them as something which confronts humanity with an episodic and serial urgency, and which resists any efforts to wrest it under control. Western rationalist culture, once believed to be capable of restraining and channelling human aggression positively, becomes exposed as a fragile crust, vulnerable to a threat from the very forces it is supposed to transcend. Infiltrated with such pessimistic assumptions, Conrad's text is undoubtedly a sign of its times; it is also a part of a wider tradition propagating a rather disquieting version of the violence mythos.

---

36   *Joseph Conrad's Letters to R.B. Cunninghame Graham*, Cedric Watts, ed., (Cambridge and New York: Cambridge University Press, 1969), 68.

37   To find out about Conrad's debt to his reading of contemporary evolutionary writing, see for example: Allan Hunter, *Joseph Conrad and the Ethics of Darwinism,* (Croom Helm: London and Canberra, 1983) and Martin Ray, "Conrad, Nordau and Other Degenerates: The Psychology of *The Secret Agent,*" *Conradiana,* (16, 1984), 125-40. For a reading of *The Secret Agent* in the light of the Second Law of Thermodynamics, see: Alan Houen, *Terrorism in Modern Literature: From Joseph Conrad to Ciaran Carson*, (Oxford: Oxford University Press, 2002), 34-92. For an analysis of *The Secret Agent* as a product of the political, social and intellectual forces of its time, see: Brian Spittles, *Joseph Conrad: Text and Context*, (London: Macmillan, 1992), 115-138.

The Author's Note advertises *The Secret Agent* as a tale dealing with "the poignant miseries and passionate credulities of a mankind always so tragically eager for self-destruction" (*SA* xxix). Violence constitutes an integral element of this narrative, and is represented in the novel in manifold ways: as a political tool and an instrument of power (Vladimir, the Professor), as an object of unhealthy fascination (the Professor, Vladimir, Karl Yundt), or as an expression of social and individual frustration (Winnie, Stevie, the Professor). Frequently motivated by a genuine hope for improving the world, it is construed as a form of dissent, a dangerous—but also most natural—reaction to reality's imperfections. As such, it acquires a tragic dimension, for disillusionment and protest seem to Conrad inherent in the human condition—after all, even so innocent a character as Stevie is prone to fits of violent abandon when faced with society's injustice and oppression. The novel's indisputable villains, the Professor and Vladimir, are both in their perverse manner guided by the courage of their convictions, trusting that the havoc they are planning to wreak will in the end do humanity a good turn. Thus, one aspect of Conrad's disturbing message is that violence cannot really be eradicated, because the wish to rebel is encoded within man's psychological makeup: each individual resembles a stick of dynamite awaiting favourable conditions to go off.

Explosive content will not metamorphose into a blast without ignition, and Conrad's text is quick to point this out. It tries to locate potential sources of danger to the modern world, "sudden holes in space and time" in which "something (generally an explosion) more or less deplorable" (*SA* 77) may take its origin. Threats are multiple, related to extreme politics and imperialist ambitions, social discontent, gender inequality, moral degeneracy, misanthropic hatred, megalomania, inappropriate application of scientific knowledge and misuse of ideology. A deadly combination of these gives the novel's universe a good shake which in a sense foreshadows the more serious upheavals of Conrad's contemporary history—momentous events already in the making or just looming on the horizon. Although *The Secret Agent* is set in the nineteenth century, it reflects tensions and anxieties peculiar to the era of its writing, capturing the *Zeitgeist* of Europe as it was slowly bracing itself for a spate of unprecedented violence, to be enacted through social and political revolutions, global conflicts, the traumas of totalitarianism and concentration camps.

The threats which Conrad's book registers are distributed among various protagonists, but most notably among the three principal agents of aggression: Vladimir, the Professor, and Winnie.[38] The first two are fanatics who mastermind explosions but do not personally

---

38   These are the three most important *noir* protagonists in Conrad's novel, but Adolf Verloc and Stevie also deserve a mention as characters implicated in violence. Not violent of their own accord, they can be easily instigated to commit brutal acts, Verloc being an immoral opportunist, and Stevie—because of his naivety. Due to the failure of his destructive mission, Stevie emerges from the narrative as a victim rather than as an aggressor, but Conrad makes it clear that he too—as a "moral creature at the mercy of his righteous passions" (*SA* 157)

commit any atrocities in the course of the novel, and the third is a hysterical murderess. Their common quality is "otherness": Vladimir is a foreigner, the Professor—a social misfit, and Winnie—a woman. All three set themselves in opposition to society, which they would like to manipulate (Vladimir), annihilate (the Professor), or simply escape (Winnie). Confronted with modern Western civilisation, (symbolised by the British metropolis), they test its braking mechanisms against violence by sowing the seeds of chaos. Though each of them does it differently and for different reasons, their dissent invariably involves an element of irrationality: Vladimir and the Professor consciously exploit the power of madness, knowing that it "alone can be truly terrifying" (*SA* 29) for contemporary society, while Winnie, submitting to a primeval murderous rage, lets herself be carried away by madness hitherto buried within her. A closer look at Conrad's figures of dread, at aspects of their aggressiveness and the motivations which guide them, will help us gain a better perspective on the problem of violence in *The Secret Agent*. It is through these subversive individuals that Conrad's version of the violence mythos receives its most elaborate exposition: they represent the uncanny otherness that encroaches upon the apparent safety of the modern world, revealing it to be a locus of terror and corruption.

England must be brought into line

Conrad's anxiety about the violent potential of the modern world is inextricably linked to his bleak political vision, his conviction that the trajectory of history has followed the wrong course and is tending towards some unimaginable catastrophe. A keen observer of contemporary political realities, Conrad was sensitive to the dangers of the moment and frequently assumed the role of Cassandra, anticipating the advancing twentieth century with its aggression and destructiveness. In his eyes, none of the many conflicting trends that were transforming European societies could guarantee a stable and secure future: social reformism, liberal democracy, the machinations of *realpolitik*, imperialism, revolution and counterrevolution all had to be dismissed as potentially threatening.[39] As early as 1905, in an essay "Autocracy and War," Conrad wrote about the dissolution of the old Europe, describing it as "an armed and trading continent, the home of slowly maturing economical contests for life and death and of loudly proclaimed world-wide

---

—is capable of violent outbursts, especially when provoked. As Carol Vanderveer Hamilton and several other critics have noted, the "delicate" retarded boy is also a would-be bomber, and thus the ultimate anarchist of the novel. See for example: Carol Vanderveer Hamilton, "Revolution from within: Conrad's natural anarchists" in: *The Conradian, Journal of the Joseph Conrad Society*, (18:2, 1994), 43.

39 Considerable evidence for this can be found in Conrad's correspondence (for example, his letters to Spiridion Kliszczewski from the years 1885-1886), and his political writing (most notably "Autocracy and War").

ambitions."[40] Voicing concern about Russian autocracy and German expansionism, he predicted a crisis in the European balance of power and the possibility of a war breaking out on the divided continent; he was also immensely sceptical about the ability of democratic governments, "without other ancestry but the sudden shout of the multitude,"[41] to avert this disaster.

Some of these fears inform *The Secret Agent*, where British democracy becomes exposed as a convenient background for international conspiracy and plots of subversion. The distinctive players here are liberalism and anarchism, and the story is about how the activity of the London underworld provokes a reaction from a foreign autocratic government. To a certain degree, the novel is a continuation of the anti-anarchist trend in the late Victorian and Edwardian literature[42] as it offers a critique of left-wing ideology and its exponents; more importantly, however, Conrad's engagement with anarchism serves as a pretext for pointing out the weaknesses of liberal rule. The London of *The Secret Agent* is characterised by a lax political climate in which the coexistence of various ideological stances may occasionally result in volatile combinations. Even though the anarchists depicted by Conrad are not dangerous in themselves (with the exception of the Professor they are all garrulous and incompetent shams), their presence invites the threat of external intervention. With its principle of indiscriminate tolerance, with the bureaucratic government represented by the likes of Sir Ethelred, and with the police indulging in cat-and-mouse encounters between legality and criminality, the British political system carries within itself the germs of self-destruction. Hospitable to all kinds of subversive individuals—foreign imperialist agents, spies, political extremists—it becomes vulnerable to undemocratic manipulation, or even to violent attack.

The representative of foreign power in Conrad's novel is Mr. Vladimir, the shady embassy official who masterminds a bomb plot against the Observatory in Greenwich. He epitomises the threat of the political "other"—a culturally different intruder, trying to transplant alien patterns of social and political organisation onto new ground. As an advocate of authoritarianism, Vladimir cannot bear Britain's "sentimental regard for individual liberty"; he thinks the country is an irritating exception to the continental rule of repression and therefore "must be brought into line" (*SA* 25). In order to sway public opinion against liberalism and shock the government into adopting more stringent policies, he conceives a propaganda stunt—a staged dynamite attack that the popular

---

40   Joseph Conrad, "Autocracy and War," in: *Notes on Life and Letters*, (The Cambridge Edition of the Works of Joseph Conrad), J.H. Stape, S.W. Reid, eds., (Cambridge: Cambridge University Press 2003), 92.

41   Conrad, "Autocracy and War," 87.

42   Among the novelists who tackled the subject of anarchism there were for example: R.L. Stevenson, Henry James, G.K. Chesterton. Most of them saw anarchism as a cultural threat and set the movement in opposition to middle class capitalist culture.

imagination will immediately ascribe to London anarchist circles. The paradox of the scheme lies in the fact that while putting it into practice, Vladimir must exploit the very features of the social order that he opposes: thanks to the liberty he enjoys in Britain, his manoeuvres may pass unnoticed. Violence which stems from international power politics can easily be disguised as a domestic affair and the general public is sure to remain oblivious to the actual forces threatening their well-being.

The vision elaborated in *The Secret Agent*, of an *arriviste* foreigner trying to change another country's politics by means of terrorist provocation and underhand dealings, may strike the reader as a conspiracy theory. However, if we look at it from the perspective of twentieth-century history, it no longer seems so improbable. The figure of Vladimir may be seen as a prophetic symbol of totalitarian regimes that were to transform Europe's future in the years to come—regimes aspiring to "bring into line" not only England but virtually the whole world. The ease with which Vladimir employs violence to achieve political aims, his belief in drastic but definitive solutions ("We don't want prevention— we want cure" (*SA* 22)), his desire to suppress civil liberties and introduce authoritarian rule acquire ominous currency in the context of events that were only two decades away from the publication of Conrad's text. The rise of totalitarianism was made possible by the application of methods that Vladimir would have approved of, including invisible government by secret services, "accentuation of unrest" (*SA* 15) and the manipulation of public fear.[43] Conrad's visionary imagination, combined with a profound understanding of the nature of politics, helped him to create a character which in many ways looks forward to the times of Soviet and Nazi oppression.

It is perhaps significant that while constructing Vladimir as an embodiment of political menace, Conrad avoids pointing to a specific government from which the danger of violence might come. Bearing in mind the writer's dislike of things Russian, numerous commentators have linked Vladimir to Muscovite autocracy, but this reading is only partly correct. As Graham McMaster argues in an essay on secrets in *The Secret Agent*, it is a deliberate ploy by Conrad to leave Vladimir's identity unclear, thus allowing for a richness of interpretation. A mixture of hints concerning the diplomat's origins produces an unsolvable puzzle: his surname and the "guttural Central Asian tones" (*SA* 31) discernible in his speech seem incompatible with the fact that his predecessors have the Teutonic-sounding names of Stott-Wartenheim and Wurmt. Similarly, the location of his embassy is shrouded in topographical mystery, as the actual London addresses of the Austrian and Russian embassies—"Chesham

---

43   For example, German and Italian fascists exploited fears of left-wing extremism in order to win political support: Mussolini's "March on Rome" was ostensibly organised to prevent a communist revolution; similarly, Hitler used the threat of a communist uprising to gain power over the Reichstag in 1933.

Place" and "Belgrave Square" are conflated into a fictional "Chesham Square" (*SA* 12). The value of such ambiguities should not be disregarded: rather than represent a single country, Vladimir stands for the imperialist ambitions exhibited by diverse political powers. He emerges from Conrad's text as an amalgam of foreign threats,[44] a presentiment of an ominous future facing Britain—and the whole of Europe—at the beginning of the twentieth century.

In terms of political commentary, the implications of the character of Vladimir are thus far more complex than it is usually assumed. His model of political activity is what Conrad finds the most unsettling among the many contemporary ideologies and forms of government: although *The Secret Agent* is crowded with revolutionaries, propagandists and all kinds of social rebels, it is at Vladimir's request that the only detonation in the novel actually takes place. He ushers in violence, endangering public safety and intruding upon the private life of the Verloc family, who will consequently be wiped off the face of the earth. Their predicament brings home to the reader the essence of Conrad's warning: that the worst type of political action is one that has no regard for individual life but is dominated by some grand vision of how society should be run. The greatest irony about Vladimir's interference into the world constructed in the novel is that while seeing himself as a figure of order, he brings disorder and destruction; his counterrevolutionary plot proves more disruptive than the revolutionary movement it is directed against. Vladimir's machinations sum up both the menace and the folly of politics which will go to any lengths to assure the predominance of a particular set of values, in reality just substituting one "tainted" cause for another.

Madness alone is truly terrifying

Conrad's reflection on how violence may function in politics is best articulated in "the philosophy of bomb throwing" (*SA* 47) that Mr. Vladimir expounds to Verloc during their secret meeting in the Embassy. For the autocratic ideologue bombs are tools, employed to achieve particular political aims; because he is not exposed to the physical effects of detonations, he can be an abstract theorist of their destructive potential. With cold-blooded calculation, he does a mental exercise in social engineering, envisaging people's reactions to anarchist bombings of various targets, and suggesting the most efficient ways of manipulating the masses:

---

44   Graham McMaster suggests that Conrad may be simultaneously alluding to the three partitioners of Poland as potential challengers of the hegemony of the British Empire, and that Vladimir's order to blow up the first meridian figuratively renders the desire to shift the balance of power in Europe and the world. See: Graham McMaster, "Some Other Secrets in *The Secret Agent*," in: *Literature and History,* (Manchester University Press, 1986), 12:2, 229-232. See also: Robert Hampson, "'Topographical Mysteries': Conrad and London," in: Gene M. Moore, ed., *Conrad's Cities: Essays for Hans van Marle,* (Amsterdam and Atlanta: Rodopi, 1992), 168-170.

[O]utrages need not be especially sanguinary . . . but they must be sufficiently startling—effective . . . An attempt upon a crowned head or on a president is sensational enough in a way, but not so much as it used to be. It has entered into the general conception of the existence of all chiefs of state. It's almost conventional—especially since so many presidents have been assassinated. Now let us take an outrage upon—say a church. Horrible enough at first sight, no doubt, and yet not so effective as a person of an ordinary mind might think. No matter how revolutionary and anarchist in inception, there would be fools enough to give such an outrage the character of a religious manifestation. And that would detract from the especial alarming significance we wish to give to the act. A murderous attempt on a restaurant or a theatre would suffer in the same way from the suggestion of non-political passion: the exasperation of a hungry man, an act of social revenge. All this is used up; it is no longer instructive as an object lesson in revolutionary anarchism. Every newspaper has ready-made phrases to explain such manifestations away . . . A bomb outrage to have any influence on public opinion now must go beyond the intention of vengeance or terrorism. It must be purely destructive. It must be that, and only that, beyond the faintest suspicion of any other object. You anarchists should make it clear that you are perfectly determined to make a clean sweep of the whole social creation. But how to get that appallingly absurd notion into the heads of the middle classes so that there should be no mistake? That's the question. By directing your blows at something outside the ordinary passions of humanity is the answer. Of course, there is art. A bomb in the National Gallery would make some noise. But it would not be serious enough. Art has never been their fetish. It's like breaking a few back windows in a man's house; whereas, if you want to make him really sit up, you must try at least to raise the roof. There would be some screaming of course, but from whom? Artists—art critics and such like—people of no account. Nobody minds what they say. But there is learning—science. Any imbecile that has got an income believes in that. (*SA* 26-29)

As Vladimir observes, in the times when anarchist attacks have become commonplace,[45] the public's susceptibility to terror has decreased: people have learnt to rationalise acts of political violence and, as a result, one cannot "count on their emotions of either pity or fear for very long" (*SA* 28). Since terrorism has an air of

---

45 Conrad's text remains in agreement with historical truth here, as indeed the high tide of militant anarchist activity in Europe occurred in the 1890s. Several heads of state fell at the hands of anarchist assassins: Sadi Carnot, the president of France in 1894, Premier Castillo of Spain in 1897, Empress Elizabeth of Austria in 1898, King Umberto of Italy in 1900, and the US President McKinley in 1901.

theatricality to it (note Vladimir's reference to its dependence on the media, as well as the mention of fear and pity—the emotions associated with Aristotle's definition of tragedy), its impact depends on the choice of a sufficiently extraordinary target. The political content is a secondary matter; what counts is the shock and awe that a demonstration evokes:

> But what is one to say to an act of destructive ferocity so absurd as to be incomprehensible, inexplicable, almost unthinkable; in fact, mad? Madness alone is truly terrifying, inasmuch as you cannot placate it either by threats, persuasion, or bribes. Moreover, I am a civilised man. I would never dream of directing you to organise a mere butchery, even if I expected the best results from it. But I wouldn't expect from a butchery the result I want. Murder is always with us. It is almost an institution. The demonstration must be against learning—science. But not every science will do. The attack must have all the shocking senselessness of gratuitous blasphemy. Since bombs are your means of expression, it would be really telling if one could throw a bomb into pure mathematics. But that is impossible. (*SA* 29)

Like a primitive priest who imposes unanimity on his audience by confronting it with some incomprehensible horror, Vladimir wants to hold a grip on the masses. In order to do this, he must activate atavistic reactions and appeal to those aspects of the modern mind that are still beyond logical control. The terrorist plan he devises is meant to deprive the public of a sense of security which rests on rational foundations: learning and science, the last values cherished by Western civilization, must prove impotent in the face of violence's "gratuitous blasphemy." The most sublime realisation of Vladimir's scheme would be a denial of the conceptually common world by "throwing a bomb into pure mathematics"; the second best possibility is an assault on Greenwich, the basis for modernity's clockwork organisation. Only an act which shatters all illusions of order and control may keep modern man in thrall so effectively that Vladimir's parody of social contract can be signed. Nothing short of madness can serve the purpose of "founding violence" for the blasé bourgeois audience: as long as reason guides their reactions, they stay indifferent to the archaic theatre of terror. In Girardian terms, Vladimir faces a society in sacrificial crisis, where the traditional methods of influencing the public no longer apply, and a need arises for some new, ultimate demonstration of power.

Vladimir's insight is echoed later on in the novel in the declarations of the Professor who himself personifies the idea of incorruptible, truly terrifying madness. In fact, all the situations in *The Secret Agent* which involve even the slightest form of violence—from Stevie's firework attack on his boss's office down to Winnie's assault on her husband— are invariably marked by insanity. H.M. Daleski sees proof of the "intense imaginative cohesion of the novel"[46] in that the bomb outrage on Greenwich, the book's central violent incident, devised by Vladimir as a demonstration of absurd ferocity is caused by the Professor's bomb carried by the half-witted Stevie. Then, its results cause Winnie to go "murdering mad" (*SA* 239) and continue the process of destruction, culminating in the final "act of madness and despair"(*SA* 282)—her own suicide.

Blood alone puts a seal on greatness

While Vladimir is an embodiment of Conrad's political fears, *The Secret Agent*'s most sinister figure—the Professor—seems to have a more universal significance. He represents violence which comes from within rather than without, a negative force stemming from the fundamentals of human nature and therefore latent in all human constructs and relations. A suicide bomber among the mass of mankind, the Professor functions as a potent symbol of inner otherness—anarchic principle which, although repressed and marginalized, may at any moment shatter the outward illusion of unity and order. As such, the Professor is arguably the most attractive of the novel's villains: pitted against the rule of the majority, he enacts the individualist dream of total rebellion, defying the logic of the society he has been born into. His fantasy of "the destruction of what is" (*SA* 279) pushes Vladimir's concept of truly terrifying madness to the extreme, but nevertheless possesses a certain appeal as it promises a cleansing change and the possibility of a fresh start. By creating the character of the Professor, Conrad exposes a difficult truth about violence: the fact that it beckons as much as it horrifies and that it can seduce us with the apparent simplicity of the solutions it offers. The novel's portrayal of the formidable anarchist is to some degree sympathetic as it acknowledges his mistrust of mankind and exasperation with the mechanisms of society,[47] but in the end the weaknesses and dangers inherent in his violent dissent become brutally unmasked. Conrad hints at the possible consequences of an attack on the foundations of civilisation and offers a critique of power which bases itself on negativity. His treatment of the Professor can be seen as a polemic with Nietzscheanism and a warning against the extreme forms that the idea of "great disengagement" may take.

The Professor emerges from Conrad's text as a man to whom violence has become a passion: all his energies are devoted to a quest for an ideal bomb that will allow him to wipe the greatest possible number of people off the face of the earth.

---

46   H.M. Daleski, *Joseph Conrad: The Way of Dispossession*, (London: Faber, 1977), 160.

47   Some critics point to an affinity between the Professor's and Conrad's own pessimistic vision of human civilisation. For example, Daphna Erdinast-Vulcan notes that "the ferocious outbursts of the mad Professor" resonate with the views of his author "at his most desperate Nietzschean—or Kurtzean—moments." See: Daphna Erdinast-Vulcan, "'Sudden Holes in Space and Time': Conrad's Anarchist Aesthetics in *The Secret Agent*," in: Gene M. Moore, ed., *Conrad's Cities: Essays for Hans van Marle*, (Amsterdam and Atlanta: Rodopi, 1992), 210-212.

A brilliant chemist, suffering from poverty and working long hours in the solitude of his tiny room which serves as his lab, he may strike us as more respectable than the "Hyperborean swine" (*SA* 193) Vladimir who enjoys all the luxuries pertaining to his diplomatic status and has people at his disposal to do the dirty work for him. The Professor's ascetic incorruptibility and perseverance seem to count in his favour, even though he applies his perverted ethics to the pursuit of a wholly unethical goal. Likewise, his intelligence is employed in the service of a mad mission, but still has the power to impress the reader. By making the Professor a devotee of science, the last fetish of modern world, Conrad creates a threatening but strangely attractive protagonist, an able man struggling against the merciless passage of time to prove the superiority of his genius, however wrongly used. As a character type, the restless bomb constructor falls somewhere between the "mad scientist" of the Gothic tradition and the unorthodox experimenters of contemporary science fiction and film, playing on our fear of modern technology and its flirt with violence. Significantly, rather than project a vision of his victory, *The Secret Agent* exposes the Professor as a supporter of a futile cause: the perfect detonator that would invest his chosen way of life with some significance stands no chance of being invented. This turns the Professor into a tragic figure and to some degree enhances his uncanny appeal, but on the other hand the reader receives a clear message that the perpetration of violence never brings the comfort of fulfilment.

Even if the Professor's mission is destined for failure, he is still Conrad's most sympathetically portrayed anarchist. Already as he makes his first appearance in the short story entitled *The Informer,* he is described as having "the true spirit of an extreme revolutionist."[48] In *The Secret Agent* he stands in stark contrast to the other conspirators—Ossipon, Michaelis and Yundt—who are just fraudulent opportunists, obsequious in the face of privilege and not truly committed to the idea of social change. Among the novel's characters, the Professor also seems to have the best, if somewhat cynical, insight into the workings of politics—a feature which has led some critics to believe that he is actually a figuration of the authorial voice.[49] Recognising revolution and legality as "counter-moves in the same game" and "forms of idleness at bottom identical" (*SA* 64), the Professor understands that true extremism has to reach beyond social convention. In a conversation with Ossipon, he dismisses the activity of the London underworld as inconclusive and suggests a more comprehensive solution to society's ills:

---

48   Joseph Conrad, "The Informer" (1908, originally published in *Harper's Magazine*, 1906), *The Complete Short Stories of Joseph Conrad*, (London: Hutchinson & Co, 1933), 489.

49   See for example the essay by Daphna Erdinast-Vulcan mentioned above, or Peter Stine, "Conrad's Secrets in *The Secret Agent*," in: *Conradiana* 13:2 (1981), 123-140.

44

[Y]ou revolutionists will never understand that. You plan the future, you lose yourselves in reveries of economical systems derived from what is; whereas what's wanted is a clean sweep and a clear start for a new conception of life. That sort of future will take care of itself if you will only make room for it. Therefore I would shovel my stuff in heaps at the corners of the streets if I had enough for that; and as I haven't, I do my best by perfecting a really dependable detonator. (*SA* 67)

Caught up in the prevalent social mechanism, the anarchists will never be able to come up with an original concept of constructive change. Only the Professor realises that in order to make a successful attack on the existing system, one must resort to methods that cannot be accounted for within the confines of that system's logic.[50] In the words of Jacques Berthoud, "justification can only exist in terms of the established norms; any rationalised policy of destruction has already surrendered to what it is trying to destroy."[51] The Professor's decision to act in a manner that Mr Vladimir would probably see as "incomprehensible, inexplicable, almost unthinkable; in fact, mad" (*SA* 29) is exactly what makes him such a menacing figure.

To be able to go against the standards of society, the Professor positions himself outside it, transcending boundaries of what is generally perceived as rational behaviour. As a potential suicide bomber, he severs his dependence on life and retreats into the realm of death, thus demonstrating his superiority over the rest of mankind:

Their character is built upon conventional morality. It leans on the social order. Mine stands free from everything artificial. They are bound in all sorts of conventions. They depend on life, which, in this connection, is a historical fact surrounded by all sorts of restraints and considerations, a complex organised fact open to attack at every point; whereas I depend on death, which knows no restraint and cannot be attacked. My superiority is evident. (*SA* 62)

The mental operation which the Professor has performed allows him to escape any form of social supervision. For example, he remains entirely beyond the reach of the law: when Ossipon suggests to him that his extremist activity is criminal, he immediately

---

50 Philosophically, the Professor's position is close to that of Nietzsche, who claimed that in order to be innovative one must transcend the boundaries of the established concepts. The idea of progress as represented by Hegel's triad is also being questioned here: a clash of opposing forces does not lead to the discovery of a new premise. For a fuller analysis of Conrad's challenging the foundations of Western thought in *The Secret Agent*, see: Jacques Darras, *Conrad and the West: Signs of Empire*, (London: Macmillan, 1982), 100-107.

51 Jacques Berthoud, "The Secret Agent," in: J.H. Stape, ed., *The Cambridge Companion to Joseph Conrad*, (Cambridge: Cambridge University Press, 1996), 114.

retorts that such categories cannot apply to him: "Criminal! What is that? What *is* crime? What can be the meaning of such an assertion?" (*SA* 69). Having convinced himself that he is immune to external threats, he becomes capable of perpetrating violence without giving society a chance to reciprocate. By means of an explosive device strapped to his own body, the Professor defies human justice: he can be eliminated at any moment, but not punished. There is nothing that could be taken away from him, not even his life, since with one squeeze of the rubber ball in his pocket he will put an end to his own existence in the manner he himself has chosen and accepted. By taking command over death, the Professor carries to extremes the anarchist principle of self-determination: he has absolute control over his fate.

At the same time, the sociopathic clarity of the Professor's vision of his own relation to society allows him to account for the mechanisms of civilisation. The reason why he successfully keeps the police at bay is society's reverence for human life: as long as his capture entails the sacrifice of innocent people, he may expect to be left in peace. The civilised world tries to avoid unnecessary bloodshed; it is equipped with institutions which are concerned with the general security of the community and whose task it is to keep violent impulses in check. There are also moral considerations against taking radical action when the least false step could have dire consequences. Such inability to set scruples aside infuriates the Professor, despite the fact that it works to his advantage as far as his personal safety is concerned. He hopes for violence to spill out, so that morality and legality would disintegrate, and the established social order would fall in ruins. As he reveals to the perplexed Ossipon, he dreams of society's deterioration into a state of total lawlessness:

> To break up the superstition and worship of legality should be our aim. Nothing would please me more than to see Inspector Heat and his likes take to shooting us down in broad daylight with the approval of the public. Half our battle would be won then; the disintegration of the old morality would have set in in its very temple. (*SA* 67)

The Professor is aware that in order to go on an anti-anarchist hunt, the police "would have to face their own institutions," which "requires uncommon grit" (*SA* 66). If those whose role is to maintain social stability could be driven to a violent abandon, it would shake people's belief in the authority of the law and help usher in the forces of chaos. The Professor's dream of "the world like shambles" (*SA* 276) might then come true: the inert British masses would discard "scrupulous prejudices" stifling their "social spirit" (*SA* 67) and begin to act spontaneously, in accordance with their will. Only then could the inadequacy of conventional cultural models become plainly visible and a revaluation of all values would be perceived as an unquestionable necessity.

Like Nietzsche, of whose views he is partly an exponent, the Professor condemns the ethical foundations of bourgeois society. The traditional morality, with all its restrictions and demands to conform, crushes the impulse for individual self-assertion and takes the side of the meek and mediocre. It leaves no room for the aristocracy of spirit, to which the Professor clearly aspires, setting himself "a goal of power and prestige to be attained without the medium of arts, graces, tact, wealth—by sheer weight of merit alone" (*SA* 73). Driven by "a frenzied puritanism of ambition" (*SA* 74), developed in the place of the abandoned religious beliefs passed on to him by his father, the Professor envisages himself as a kind of *Übermensch*. He wants to play the role of a "moral agent" (*SA* 74) who will restore mankind's reverence for the natural virtues of courage and strength. For that reason, he insists that power must first be wrestled from the hands of the earth's "sinister masters—the weak, the flabby, the silly, the cowardly, the faint of heart and the slavish of mind" (*SA* 276). His cure for the disease of decadence that troubles modern society is terrible in its simplicity: elimination of those inferior creatures who, being strong in their number, stand in the way of higher men. The tirade in which he discloses his views to Ossipon is noticeably marked with genocidal fury:

> Exterminate, exterminate! That is the only way of progress. It is! Follow me, Ossipon. First the great multitude of the weak must go, then the only relatively strong. You see? First the blind, the deaf and the dumb, then the halt and the lame—and so on. Every taint, every vice, every prejudice, every contention must meet its doom. (*SA* 276)

In his plans to overturn the traditional social organisation, the Professor does not consider the possibility of using non-violent methods of argumentation; he is deeply convinced that "the framework of an established social order cannot be effectually shattered except by some form of collective or individual violence" (*SA* 74). He sees violence as the driving force of history: his belief that "blood alone puts a seal on greatness" (*SA* 277) reduces his perception of civilisation's development to a series of barbaric acts. Even his contemporary political system has been introduced through bloodshed—although, paradoxically, its aim was supposedly to ensure the peaceful coexistence of various social classes. "The condemned social order has not been built up on paper and ink, and I don't fancy that a combination of paper and ink will ever put an end to it, whatever you may think," (*SA* 65-66) he tells Ossipon, disclosing before him a vision of the violent change to come. With explosives as his means of communication, the Professor considers himself the only person deserving the name of propagandist. Unfortunately, his policy of general destruction is not accompanied by any sort of political programme. Like most fanatics, the restless bomb constructor wants only to wipe out the present society but has no clear vision as to what could come in its place. When Ossipon asks him what will remain after all the imperfect representatives of the human race have been exterminated, he hears the reply: "I remain—if I am strong enough" (*SA* 276).

The word "I" is the key to the Professor's lethal extremism: the propaganda by the deed he espouses serves nothing else but his bruised ego. Although the narrative repeatedly refers to him as "the Perfect Anarchist" (*SA* 75, 87, 112, 275, 277), the designation is only justified in terms of psychology, not politics. A bitter man, who had every chance to become a scientist but abandoned academia and all his later occupations due to what he perceived as "unfair treatment" (*SA* 68), the Professor takes revenge on a society that has failed to appreciate his merits. Motivated by personal grudges, he is a mock-Nietzschean hero: in his professed rebellion against the established values he fails to act as a genuine *Übermensch*, because he stops at nihilism, being able to destroy but not to create. His behaviour is a classic example of resentment; denied power and prestige, he seeks to prove himself worthy of them:

> By exercising his [moral] agency with ruthless defiance he procured for himself the appearances of power and personal prestige. That was undeniable to his vengeful bitterness. It pacified its unrest; and in their own way the most ardent of revolutionaries are perhaps doing no more but seeking for peace in common with the rest of mankind - the peace of soothed vanity, of satisfied appetites, or perhaps of appeased conscience. (*SA* 74)

Additionally, the Professor may be seen as a caricature of any individualist who places himself in opposition to the crowd and craves rejection from it, only to deify himself.[52] His greatest fear, presented by Conrad as perfectly well-founded, is that the mass of mankind will remain indifferent: "What if nothing could move them? Such moments come to all men whose ambition aims at a direct grasp upon humanity—to artists, politicians, thinkers, reformers, or saints." (*SA* 75)

On closer inspection, the Professor's anarchism turns out to be a cover-up for misanthropy and megalomania—two qualities which in a fatal combination are likely to generate violence (as twentieth-century history was quick to prove, Conrad was endowed with remarkable intuition). Fortunately, despite the Professor's confidence in his ability to spread death and destruction, his potential is revealed to have its limits. He can only act as an "I," as an individual, and for that reason he will never be able to realise his dream of sending the whole of mankind to a collective doom. Resolving to work alone and treating with contempt the activity of his anarchist comrades, he embraces "sinister loneliness" and stands helpless before "the resisting power of numbers, the unattackable stolidity of a great multitude" (*SA* 87).

---

52   William A. Johnsen sees this kind of wish as a perversion of the ancient sacrificial mechanism. Because in modern times the focus of attention has shifted onto the figure of the victim, unjustly ostracised, some individuals willingly place themselves in this position in order to assert their superiority over others, whom they imagine as vulgar and unperceptive. See: William A. Johnsen, *Violence in Modernism: Ibsen, Joyce, Woolf,* (Gainesville: University Press of Florida, 2003), 41.

The Professor's pretences to greatness are further confirmed as self-delusions through the sharp bite of satire with which he is being described. The narrative ruthlessly undermines him by drawing the reader's attention to his physical imperfections and mental weaknesses. Ossipon, who analyses most characters in the novel in the light of Lombroso's theory,[53] finds in the Professor numerous symptoms of degeneracy, such as frail skull, sloping forehead, unhealthy complexion, protruding ears, bad eyesight, and "lamentable inferiority of the whole physique" (*SA* 57)—features which would definitely weaken his chances for survival, were he to find himself in the "world like shambles" of his dreams. Similarly Inspector Heat, whom the Professor treats with particular disdain, sees through his mask of the ultimate anarchist. Knowing that the Professor mobilises all his hatred against the mass of humanity, Heat takes pleasure in reminding him that mankind may prove too multitudinous to be destroyed by a single blast: "You'll find we are too many for you" (*SA* 87).

Despite the satirical treatment the Professor receives over the course of the novel, he still adds an air of menace to the plot and is perhaps one of the most memorable of all Conrad's characters. To some degree, his charismatic quality derives from his exotic attempt to domesticate death, which itself has been a subject of humanity's perennial fascination. Yet the figure of the Professor also takes on an archetypal significance: he can be treated as an embodiment of the destructive potential latent in all human communities, and in all human beings. The frail body of a suicide bomber melting into the metropolitan crowd in the closing scene of *The Secret Agent* symbolises the forces of anarchy endemic to any form of social organisation and exposes the fragility of man's illusion of safety. "Averting his eyes from the odious multitude of mankind," the Professor passes on "unsuspected and deadly, like a pest in the street full of men" (*SA* 283). The double meaning of the word "pest" perfectly renders the ambivalence with which we can interpret the Professor's role in the novel: on the one hand, he is insignificant like vermin, a contemptible maniac causing nuisance to society, but on the other he resembles a pestilence, carrying the germs of violence and infecting fellow beings with his bloodthirsty nihilism.

She was not a submissive creature

Just as the Professor is a delayed-release bomb among the mass of unsuspecting Londoners, Winnie Verloc functions as an undetected explosive in a bourgeois household. Her accumulated frustration results in what Peter Conrad aptly terms "a seismic upheaval

---

53   Ossipon is an advocate of biological determinism as propagated in the nineteenth century by the Italian criminologist Cesare Lombroso (1835-1909). Lombroso maintained that criminals displayed hereditary "atavistic" traits, and that therefore by looking for facial features he deemed "atavistic," criminal tendencies could be weeded out of the population. Conrad's engagement with Lombroso's theory in *The Secret Agent* has been discussed by Allan Hunter in Chapter Five of *Joseph Conrad and the Ethics of Darwinism* (Croom Helm: London and Canberra, 1983).

in a cramped suburban room,"[54] the novel's second detonation and a far-flung effect of the blast which killed Stevie. The plot of *The Secret Agent* eventually emerges as being "Mrs Verloc's story" (in accordance with the author's intention) when the seemingly unremarkable, self-denying woman transforms into a figure of dread, outstripping in destructive frenzy all the self-styled anarchists who used to meet secretly in her husband's shop. She epitomises the whole troubled potential of Conrad's book as her inner pressures explode into violence, completing the disintegration of what had seemed a stable and respectable world. In terms of poetic justice, the murder Winnie commits may be seen as a fitting retribution for the sacrificed child, yet as an aggressive outburst in its own right it acquires various other functions in the text, one of them being to assert the dangerous energy of the modern female. Like many novelists of the period, Conrad focuses his attention on the woman as the site of hitherto unacknowledged perverse passions. If, as Lee Horsley suggests, *The Secret Agent* is an early realisation of the *noir* convention, then Winnie is the novel's *femme fatale*, violently freeing herself from a confining relationship with a man who has abused his power.

By turning Winnie into a murderess of the patriarch, Conrad addresses important aspects of the violence mythos in Western culture, including the popular beliefs about male aggression and female subordination, the opinion that women are unable to transcend instinctual urges, the view of feminine anger as irrational and hysterical, and the mistrust of the woman as "Other."[55] Although most of these assumptions are in the end upheld rather than contested, *The Secret Agent*—as a comment on gender antagonism—is a meaningful contribution to the wider cultural discourse of its time. The novel acknowledges, not without sympathy, women's frustration with the social, domestic and economic constraints imposed on them by the patriarchal world order; it also construes femininity as a subversive force capable of violent revolt, anticipating in this way the sex war and the subsequent revision of gender roles which was to take place in the first decades of the twentieth century.

Winnie's crime occurs during a domestic dispute, but it can be interpreted in much broader terms, since in *The Secret Agent* the political is the personal and the personal is the political. Trapped in a marriage of convenience with a man who was supposed to provide for her, her mother and, most importantly, her retarded brother, Winnie is a classic example of late-Victorian (and perhaps also Edwardian) womanhood. In order to secure a decent future for her family, she has made a series of painful sacrifices, including parting with the love of her young life. She views her

---

54 Conrad, *Modern Times*, 220.

55 About the relation between violence and gender in Western culture, see: Whitmer, *The Violence Mythos*, 12-13 and 39-43.

relationship with Verloc as a transaction: in return for the financial stability which guarantees Stevie's welfare she acts as a paragon of solicitude and offers her husband marital bliss. Verloc, for his part, takes his domestic tranquillity for granted, assuming that he is "loved for himself" (*SA* 229), and treating Winnie "with the regard one has for one's chief possession" (*SA* 164). Like many marital unions in Conrad's time, the Verlocs' marriage is a conventional arrangement, founded on deception and plagued by mutual incomprehension. Its continuation is only possible thanks to a strategy of avoidance, and the mechanical performance of the roles ascribed to one's social position, without ever questioning their sense:

> Their accord was perfect, but it was not precise. It was a tacit accord, congenial to Mrs Verloc's incuriosity and to Mr. Verloc's habits of mind, which were indolent and secret. They refrained from going to the bottom of facts and motives. (*SA* 224)

Things begin to go wrong when Verloc unwittingly violates what Winnie understands as the fundamental condition of their contract: death brought by him on Stevie cancels the many years of her heroic self-denial. Winnie's disappointment is symbolic of the fate of numerous women economically dependent on men, doomed to wither in unfulfilling relationships without any guarantee that the stabilisation they had craved for would eventually be granted to them. Thus, *The Secret Agent* queries the institution of marriage from the viewpoint of the disadvantaged female, making it clear that women do have legitimate social grievances and that they are frequently victimised by their family situation.

Along with the unveiling of the gloomy realities of bourgeois domesticity, Conrad's text voices anxiety about a possible backlash against patriarchal domination. Challenging the popular stereotype of women as meek and malleable, the novel warns against the possibility of their violent awakening and sudden transformation from victims into victimisers. The Verlocs' final encounter in Chapter Eleven rehearses a scary scenario, showing what may happen when female patience snaps: a kitchen knife landing unexpectedly in Verloc's chest marks the end of what has turned out to be an unfair deal. As Brian Spittles rightly points out, at the moment of killing her husband Winnie does not act as an individual, but functions "an archetype of female repression,"[56] an embodiment of anger that has been harboured for centuries:

> Into that plunging blow, delivered over the side of the couch, Mrs Verloc had put all the inheritance of her immemorial and obscure descent, the simple ferocity of the age of caverns, and the unbalanced nervous fury of the age of bar-rooms. (*SA* 239)

---

56 Spittles, *Joseph Conrad: Text and Context*, 136-7.

Thus, exhausted with her role of "an angel of the hearth," the woman becomes a menacing presence, a secret agent, and—to use the expression of Carol Vanderveer Hamilton—"a natural anarchist," whose psyche is so constructed that it cannot bear injustice and exploitation.[57]

Significantly, Conrad's archetypal conservative male, the pig-like Verloc, remains completely oblivious to his wife's subversive potential. Too complacent to register the change that Winnie undergoes after the loss of Stevie, which to him is merely a "lamentable" incident (*SA* 220), he behaves like a shallow, disparaging buffoon until the last moment of his life. Throughout the build-up to the murder, during the long scene that unfolds over 23 pages, Verloc underestimates the extent of Winnie's suffering; rather, his incorrigible egoism leads him to expect the usual affection and emotional support from her. Confronted with her grief, he feels "resigned in a truly marital spirit" (*SA* 236) and tries to cope with the situation by resorting to the traditional repertoire of simplistic formulas, offering the following pieces of advice: "You go to bed now. What you want is a good cry" (*SA* 219); "You must pull yourself together"(*SA* 225); "Rest and quiet's what you want" (*SA* 230). Yet the woman whom Verloc addresses with such familiarity has already estranged herself from him—she wears a black veil over "a still unreadable face" (*SA* 234) and seems to be an alien creature, "a masked and mysterious visitor of impenetrable intentions" (*SA* 233). When the undiscouraged male tries to squeeze her back into the old mould and, disregarding the trauma she is experiencing, requests domestic and sexual favours, he earns a violent response. The sad part of the story is that as he draws his last breath before Winnie's knife meets its destination, the only explanation he can conjure up for his wife's behaviour is that she has "gone raving mad—murdering mad" (*SA* 239). He dies ignorant of the causes of her frustration, finding it easier to dismiss her as insane rather than acknowledge his guilt. Conrad denies him even this final moment of recognition: very consistently, Verloc perpetuates the Western model of patriarchal prejudice which sees female anger and violence as unjustified, resulting from a gender-determined deficiency of rationality.[58]

To some extent, Conrad is guilty of a similar simplification: his novel may acknowledge women's exasperation with their disadvantaged position in the family and society, but the portrayal of Winnie as a violent figure is by no means free from gender stereotyping. Compared with *The Secret Agent*'s male villains, Vladimir and the Professor, Winnie does not seem to be using her brain when perpetrating violence—instead, she acts according to the dictates of her maternal sensibility. There is no element of calculation in her murder of Verloc, committed on the spur of the moment and in an altered state of mind,

---

57   Vanderveer Hamilton, "Revolution from within: Conrad's natural anarchists," 43.

58   See: Whitmer, *The Violence Mythos*, 13.

after her "moral nature had been subjected to a shock of which, in the physical order, the most violent earthquake of history could only be a faint and languid rendering" (*SA* 233). Winnie's "militant love" (*SA* 225) for Stevie is an extenuating circumstance in terms of the ethical assessment of her deed; at the same time, however, it reduces her to the level of an animal, a lioness defending one of her cubs. Instincts and emotions come to the fore as the main factors motivating female behaviour: guided by "maternal and violent" (*SA* 220) impulses, the woman emerges from Conrad's text as fundamentally antithetical to the coldly rational man. If she demonstrates her anger, it is because she has lost control over her anarchic inner essence and because her reactions are biologically conditioned. Ultimately, then, *The Secret Agent* subscribes to one of the basic value judgements within the Western violence mythos, pronouncing aggression as normal and intentional in men while abnormal and uncontrollable in women.

The pathos of female violence is further emphasised by the novel's finale, in which we observe Winnie spinning towards complete psychological disintegration and suicide. As it turns out, Conrad's heroine cannot do anything with the freedom she gains after killing Verloc: although her assault on the conservative male world brings her a momentary peace of mind, the feeling of relief quickly gives way to a panicked realisation of the possible consequences of her act. Consumed by the fear of punishment, Winnie is unable to transcend the limitations imposed by the society in which she lives; unlike Vladimir or the Professor, who place themselves beyond legality and dream up alternative worlds, she never aspires to a Nietzschean pose of a creator of values. Apart from getting rid of Verloc, Winnie has no long-term goals and no clear concept of her future as a "free woman" (*SA* 231, 232, 238, 240—the novel's narrator repeatedly refers to her in this way, ironically underscoring the illusory nature of the sense of release she experiences). Like a bird which has lived all its life in captivity, Winnie quickly discovers that she cannot function outside the cage: at the first opportunity that arises, she denies her newly gained identity by making herself dependent on a man. Her mistakes are repeated as she puts her trust in Ossipon and suffers another betrayal, after which she can escape only into death.

Winnie's desperate manoeuvres before she actually throws herself into the river are prompted by a belated reflection on the precariousness of her position. It is only upon awakening from a murderous trance that she is able to see her deed in a wider context:

> Mrs Verloc was no longer a person of leisure and responsibility. She was afraid. . . . Mrs Verloc, who always refrained from looking deep into things, was compelled to look into the very bottom of this thing. She saw there no haunting face, no reproachful shade, no vision of remorse, no sort of ideal conception. She saw there an object. That object was the gallows. Mrs Verloc was afraid of the gallows.

<blockquote>
She was terrified of them ideally. . . . Mrs Verloc, though not a well-informed woman, had a sufficient knowledge of the institutions of her country to know that gallows are no longer erected romantically on the banks of dismal rivers or on wind-swept headlands, but in the yards of jails. There within four high walls, as if into a pit, at dawn of day, the murderer was brought out to be executed, with a horrible quietness and, as the reports in the newspapers always said, "in the presence of the authorities." With her eyes staring on the floor, her nostrils quivering with anguish and shame, she imagined herself all alone amongst a lot of strange gentlemen in silk hats who were calmly proceeding about the business of hanging her by the neck. That—never! Never! And how was it done? The impossibility of imagining the details of such quiet execution added something maddening to her abstract terror. The newspapers never gave any details except one, but that one with some affectation was always there at the end of a meagre report. Mrs Verloc remembered its nature. It came with a cruel burning pain into her head, as if the words "The drop given was fourteen feet" had been scratched on her brain with a hot needle. "The drop given was fourteen feet." (SA 244-245)
</blockquote>

The act of assertive energy which Winnie has performed is not to be tolerated in an organised society that has developed mechanisms to protect itself from violent individuals. Having escaped Verloc's dominance, Winnie has no chance to escape the violence of the state (and unlike the Professor, she does not readily embrace the prospect of death). Interestingly, she perceives her failure primarily in terms of gender oppression, associating "the institutions of her country" with "gentlemen in silk hats . . . calmly proceeding about the business of hanging her by the neck" (SA 245). It dawns on her that the patriarchal world she has struck against will exact a violent retribution in the majesty of the law, and that she will be ruthlessly executed as a rebel against the "silk hat" civilisation. In contrast to the hysteria of her outburst, the male response will be calm and confident, sanctioned by the authority of the legal system designed to protect male power.

It has been the subject of critical debate whether Conrad's decision to let Winnie die a suicidal death is a mark of his sensitivity to the gender dimension of her deed. Eileen Sypher, for example, reads The Secret Agent as a thoroughly misogynistic text where the narrator must kill Winnie off because she epitomises the anarchic potential of femininity.[59] Developing this thought, one might argue that the act of taking her own life is a confirmation of Winnie's irrationality, an ultimate proof of women's inability to control and govern themselves. On the other hand, Winnie's suicide may be seen as a demonstration of defiance: killing herself is the only possible means that she has in order

---

59   Eileen Sypher, "Anarchism and Gender: James's The Princess Casamassima and Conrad's The Secret Agent," Henry James Review 9:1 (1998), 1-16.

to escape patriarchal domination, and so she prefers to drown in the Thames rather than let gentelmen in silk hats lay their hands on her. Like many murderers of modernist fiction, she cannot be expected to live on—it might be interpreted as a silent approval of her drastic action, and this is something that the moralist Conrad would not allow. However, as Arthur Redding observes, the tragic end Winnie faces endows her with "a certain magnificence," whether in accordance with, or against Conrad's intentions:

> If Conrad is condemned to murder possibility in the figure of Winnie, as a "character," she nonetheless outmanoeuvers the condemnation of her creator. In fact, Winnie becomes the stereotypical "tragic figure" of the novel, for it is she and only she—not Stevie, not Verloc—who comes to a fully conscious realization of the forces arrayed against her. And she lashes out against them, certainly with more efficient force than a more recognized figure such as Kate Chopin's Edna Pontellier. At least she takes one of the bastards down with her when she goes.[60]

Simple ferocity of the age of caverns

Winnie's aggressive outburst may be related to the turn-of-the-century gender politics, but it is also possible to view it more generally as a manifestation of the shadowy underside of modern experience. In its portrayal of violence, *The Secret Agent* returns to questions already explored in *Heart of Darkness*, namely the distance between civilisation and savagery and the possibility of a sudden atavistic regression. Conrad's imagination is again captured by the idea of "the primitive mind," slumbering in some unreformed recess of the modern psyche and awaiting its opportunity to run riot. This time, the threat of primeval anarchy becomes located in two seemingly harmless protagonists—a middle class woman and a backward child. In both of them, the control of reason proves insufficient to restrain the "simple ferocity" (*SA* 239) awakening on a sudden impulse and turning them into potential murderers. Even though their anger may appear morally righteous, as it is inspired by the injustices of the society they live in, the uncivilised behaviour in which it finds expression is invariably subject to critique. Conrad seems to suggest that by following primitive drives humans can only bring misery upon themselves and that the traditional social order, despite its imperfections, serves as a braking mechanism against the outbreak of primeval chaos. Although *The Secret Agent* does not openly celebrate the "holy terror of scandal and gallows and lunatic asylums,"[61] the conviction that civilisation serves the best interests of humanity is still

---

60   Redding, *Raids on Human Consciousness*, 126-127.
61   Joseph Conrad, *Heart of Darkness*, (Ware: Wordsworth Classics, 1995), 49.

very much there. In this respect, Conrad consistently goes against the general tenor of modernism: rather than support the Nietzschean and Freudian dream of freeing the instincts repressed by the civilising process, he speaks in favour of the disappearing values that used to bind communities together.

The Secret Agent associates the threat of violence with madness, that is, the suspension of rational control. Situations in which characters rely on instinctual reactions fall into this category and are therefore perceived as potentially detrimental. For example, Stevie's fits of violent rage, during which he sets off fireworks in the office, or grabs the kitchen knife by way of protest against injustice and oppression, are presented not as just naive but harmful. Stevie is an embodiment of the passionate simplicity that operates according to the ancient principle of "an eye for an eye, a tooth for a tooth." Worked up by stories of human depravity, he grows homicidal and can be used, by a cynical bully like Verloc, to plant a bomb, without ever apprehending the irony of correcting evil with evil. Similarly his sister, when the extremity of her suffering releases her "from all earthly ties" (*SA* 229) and lifts the normal inhibitions of culture, suddenly becomes capable of murder. She commits her crime in a Stevie-like state of moral limbo—a condition that Conrad emphasises by depicting her with changed facial features, suggestive of some thanatonic union between her and the retarded boy:

> As if the homeless soul of Stevie had flown for shelter straight to the breast of his sister, guardian, and protector, the resemblance of her face with that of her brother grew at every step, even to the droop of the lower lip, even to the slight divergence of the eyes. (*SA* 239)

As Conrad repeatedly makes clear, at the moment of killing Verloc Winnie takes a step back in evolution. Apart from regressing mentally to the level of Stevie, she is described as enacting the murder from "the age of caverns," supported by "all the inheritance of her immemorial and obscure descent" (*SA* 239). The human past that comes alive within her can hardly be called noble: its legacy amounts to a perfectly developed killer instinct. Drawing on the reserves of violent energy stored during primitive times, Winnie stabs at Verloc with unbelievable precision. Almost like a beast of prey, she momentarily attains mastery over her body and nerves:

> She commanded her wits now, her vocal organs; she felt herself to be in an almost preternaturally perfect control of every fibre of her body. . . . She was clear-sighted. She had become cunning. . . . She was unhurried. Her brow was smooth. (*SA* 238)

By drawing attention to Winnie's concentration and composure, Conrad seems to embrace the social Darwinist view which treats aggression as biologically conditioned and natural in human beings. Although centuries of civilised conduct have helped to curb and repress violent urges, the savage lurking beneath the decorous façade can be easily accessed and the whole history of human moral achievement undone in an instant. However, as Winnie's example testifies, apart from a fleeting sense of regained primeval vitality, there are few benefits to be drawn from a return to savagery. The shadow self discovered by Winnie while taking her irrevocable step ultimately works against her: the blood trickling on the floor as she lets her knife go unleashes a "destroying flood" (*SA* 241) in which she must drown. Like Kurtz in *Heart of Darkness*, she is ill-advised by her primitive instincts and reaches a point of no return.

A victim to the enemy within—the corrupt human nature—Winnie completes the gallery of villains in *The Secret Agent*. She is one of the many secret agents in the monstrous town of Conrad's vision where there is "darkness enough to bury five million of lives" (*SA* xxxi). When the novel closes, we have no doubt that the sinister potential of the urban graveyard has by no means exhausted itself and that the mysterious forces operating in it will surely engulf many more than just the Verloc family.

In the Author's Note preceding the novel Conrad declares that "in telling Winnie Verloc's story to its anarchistic end of utter desolation, madness and despair, and telling it as I have told it, I have not intended to commit a gratuitous outrage of the feelings of mankind" (*SA* xxxiii). As the novel unfolds caustically and its message comes as compact as the bomb attack on the Greenwich Observatory of 1894, it becomes increasingly difficult to believe the author's declarations. We may wish to recoil from Conrad's anatomisation of the modern world's propensity for violence but we cannot deny its persuasiveness, especially when reading *The Secret Agent* with the benefit of hindsight afforded by the knowledge of both twentieth century history and contemporary political reality.

CHAPTER III

"All Personality Was Catching"—Mimetic Rivalry and the Contagion of Violence in *Tarr*

> Alas! The time is coming when man will no longer give birth to stars.
>
> Alas! The time of the most contemptible man is coming, one who can no longer despise himself.
>
> Behold! I show you the last man.
>
> . . . His race is as ineradicable as the flea-beetle; the last man lives longest.
>
> No shepherd and one herd! Everybody wants the same, everybody is the same...
>
> Friedrich Nietzsche, *Thus Spoke Zarathustra*

In the same year in which Conrad published *The Secret Agent*, Wyndham Lewis, then a member of the internationalist artistic coterie of Montparnasse, came up with an idea for what was to become the novel *Tarr*. It began as a short story of the duel and death of a German student in Paris, and then developed in Conradian fashion, gradually acquiring new characters and episodes, and becoming more of a critique of the bohemian style of life. Revised a number of times over a span of eight years, the book changed along with Lewis's interest in literary creation—as well as with the times in which it was being written— eventually evolving into an unsettling commentary on the cultural crisis of modernity. Completed long before *Ulysses* and other works which would come to form the high modernist canon, at the time of its publication *Tarr* was in many respects a ground-breaking novel whose pioneering attempt to render the realities of what was essentially a build-up to the Great War gave Lewis the right to call it "the first book of an epoch in England."[62]

---

62 Wyndham Lewis, Preface to the 1928 edition of *Tarr*, reprinted in the 2010 edition by Scott W. Klein, (Oxford: Oxford University Press, 2010), 3.

In many respects, *Tarr* links up well with Conrad's *noir* thriller: like *The Secret Agent*, it explores the wasteland theme against the menacing background of a modern metropolis, this time Paris rather than London, where "the unscrupulous heroes chase each other's shadows," "largely ignorant of all but their restless personal lives" (*T* 21). In place of sham anarchists and spies Lewis substitutes sham artists and intellectuals, belonging to a community of "bourgeois-bohemians" (*T* 127)—a strange hybrid of subversive aspirations and middle-class calculativeness. Once more, wastrelism, male sexism, habitual falsehood, inertia, alienation and a general sense of meaninglessness are castigated as society's chief maladies, plaguing even those who should be able to resist the "herd mentality." Although Lewis's novel does not gesture towards a politically engaged mode of writing, or towards existential anguish characteristic of the *noir* convention, the judgement it passes on modernity is very much like that of Conrad's. The fictional worlds of *Tarr* and *The Secret Agent* are separated by a gap of a few decades, but affected by similar crisis symptoms: a dehumanisation of social and personal relationships, a lack of communication, and a decline of moral standards. Behind the ever thinner polite façade, Lewis, too, finds only hostility, deception and intrigue; his civilised protagonists are "sicknesses for each other" (*T* 72), working towards mutual destruction or degradation. The only difference is the intensity of the social malaise and the degree to which it has been recognised: what in Conrad's text remained restricted to the underworld, in *Tarr* resurfaces in polite society and among the supposed intellectual and artistic elite.

Like Conrad, Lewis apprehends the forces of chaos arrayed against the human illusion of order. However, in investigating the violence latent in human beings and human communities, he does not content himself with a recognition that it is simply there, ticking like a bomb. What interests him is the context and the manner in which violence is engendered, allowed to flourish and then spread. He wants to know about the process rather that the product, focusing primarily on the specific combination of social circumstances and individual inclinations that make aggressive interactions possible. Such an approach is perhaps understandable if we take into account the historical timing of Lewis's most creative period of work on the novel, that is, the years immediately before and after the outbreak of the Great War. The temporal proximity of this liminal event may have directed Lewis's attention to the causes of violence: counted among the earliest of the World War I fictions, *Tarr* is in a way one of the first attempts at looking back on the sacrificial crisis that culminated in a global catastrophe on hitherto unknown scale.

As Lewis admits in his autobiography *Blasting and Bombardiering*, the Great War's gestation period had a formative influence on his development and became unwittingly reflected in his work:

You will be astonished to find how like art is to war, I mean "modernist art." They talk a lot about how a war just finished effects art. But you will learn here how a war *about to start* can do the same thing. I have set out to show how war, art, civil war, strikes and coup d'états dovetail into each other.

It is somewhat depressing to consider how as an artist one is always holding the mirror up to politics without knowing it. . . . A prophet is a most unoriginal person: all he is doing is imitating something that is not there, but soon will be. With me war and art have been mixed from the start.[63]

Imbued with the spirit of the times, Tarr bore, upon its completion in 1915, a striking relevance to the contemporary political situation. The novel's vision of a diseased world, with its international collection of expatriates indulging in mutual antagonism, gained a new significance in the context of a global armed conflict. Lewis himself must have been taken aback by the accuracy of his premonitions, as he thought it necessary to explain in the Epilogue to his book that the figure of the "disagreeable German," Otto Kreisler, had not been invented for the purposes of war propaganda. At the same time, he found his protagonist "very apposite" (*T* 13) and suggested that the developments on the Western Front might actually help to illustrate his fictional creation.[64]

Even though certain implications in *Tarr* may have gone beyond the author's original intent, the tale may easily be seen in terms of an anatomy of the epoch in which the upheaval of 1914-1918 had its complicated roots. In its attempt to analyse aggression, it captures negative energies at work in the patriarchal, bourgeois society of pre-war Europe and hints at the possibility of their violent eruption. The world depicted in the novel is inherently flawed, eroded by a tide of frustration which results from the growing disillusionment with conventional cultural models and values. Despite pretences to greatness, the civilisation of "white men, strong men, super men; 'great statesmen,' 'great soldiers,' 'great artists,' 'sacred faith,' 'noble pity,' 'sacrifice,' 'pure art,' 'abstract

---

63   Wyndham Lewis, *Blasting and Bombardiering*, 4.

64   The opening fragment of Lewis's statement runs as follows: "This book was begun eight years ago; so I have not produced this disagreeable German for the gratification of primitive partisanship aroused by the war. On the other hand, having had him up my sleeve for so long, I let him out at this moment in the undisguised belief that he is very apposite. . . . The myriads of Prussian germs, gases, and gangrenes, released into the air and for the past year obsessing everything, revived my quiescent creation. I was moved to vomit Kreisler forth. It is one big germ more. May the flames of Louvain help to illuminate (and illustrate) my hapless protagonist! His misdemeanours too, which might appear too harshly real at ordinary times, have, just now, too obvious confirmations to be questioned."(*T* 13) "The Epilogue" is dated November 1915, but was first published in the Novemeber 1917 issue of *The Egoist*, in the serialised, abridged version of *Tarr*. In the book edition the statement was converted into a "Prologue"; in Paul O'Keeffe's edition of the 1918 version of *Tarr* it is called a "Preface" and placed at the beginning of the novel.

art'" (*T* 26) has, in the eyes of the title protagonist, Frederick Tarr, utterly exhausted itself. Assumptions that once constituted the core of Western culture have degenerated into a set of empty phrases, serving as a cover-up for moral and spiritual desolation. The void that opens up before modern man becomes a central issue for Lewis: his book anticipates, in the fateful arc of Kreisler's life and in the muddled existence of the remaining characters, the potential outcome of this condition.

Placed in the context of a mentality change related to the advent of the commodity culture, *Tarr* constructs a vivid picture of what Dennis Brown terms "the raw energy of twentieth-century capitalism."[65] It is against this background that violence is engendered: trends of modern society prove conducive to the corruption of personality, which in turn leads to deviant behaviour and aggression. By portraying a society lacking a spiritual axis, *Tarr* shows how frustration, unfulfilled desire and exaggerated ambition unleash destructive forces which ultimately turn against those who yield to their powerful pull.

With its systematic, almost scientifically dispassionate interest in the problem of violence, *Tarr* resembles a psychological case study: a detailed analysis of one character whose experience serves to provide insight into the mechanisms generating and fuelling aggression. Focusing on an individual's entanglement with primitive, instinctive drives, which eventually prove more powerful than civilised reason, the novel offers a caustic commentary on human baseness and inadequacy. It recognises violence as a social plague and exposes the ease with which people succumb to mimetic pressures by reciprocating the negativity of others.

Doomed, evidently

Lewis's attempt to portray how violence originates in frustration and deprivation is clearly visible in the life story of Otto Kreisler, who enters the world of bourgeois-bohemians already carrying the stigma of failure. He arrives in Paris laden with the burden of an unsatisfactory past, which can be summed up as a headlong flight from responsibility: the trail of problems he has left behind includes unpaid debts in Rome, "offspring throughout Germany" (*T* 94), both acknowledged and unacknowledged, as well as several unhappy liasons with women, full of "misunderstandings and wistful separations" (*T* 102). Among the latter, the marriage of Kreisler's ex-fiancée to his own father constantly fuels his sense of frustration and despair, as it has not only made his family relations difficult, but also affected his financial well-being.

---

65   Dennis Brown, *Intertextual Dynamics within the Literary Group—Joyce, Lewis, Pound and Eliot. The Men of 1914,* (London: Macmillan, 1990), 68.

Apart from being entangled in an oedipal drama, Kreisler is a social parasite, who at the age of thirty-six has not moved beyond the status of art student. Since he does not seem to be endowed with much talent—"he has only lost one picture so far" (*T* 81)—he cannot make a living out of his creative work. For many years, he was provided for by others, mainly his father who used to send subsidies regularly, but also by wealthy sponsors like Ernst Volker, for whom Kreisler's "inertia and phlegm . . . were a charm and something to be envied" (*T* 93). Encouraged to treat his passivity as an asset, Kreisler has accepted wastrelism as a mode of existence and is interested exclusively in easy money.[66] The idea of becoming self-sufficient is alien to him: when Kreisler Senior (whose budget, presumably, is strained by the cost of maintaining a young wife) grows disaffected with his son's indolence and offers him a post in a commercial concern, he is met with an adamant refusal. Even the threat of a reduction, and prospectively a cessation, of the monthly allowance cannot force Kreisler to change his ways; he would rather commit suicide than yield to his father's conditions. With increased determination, he clings to his parasitical lifestyle by running up debts, scrounging and pawning his possessions. His move to Paris is part of his survival strategy: he hopes that a "reopening of his account with little friend Ernst," admittedly, "a most delicate business" (*T* 87), will pull him out of his dire straits.

And indeed his hopes appear both reasonable and justified: by virtue of his vices he seems to be a perfect addition to the superficial society of Parisian expatriates. As a wastrel and a pleasure-seeking man, ready to exploit others to achieve his own ends, he seems predestined to thrive among the bogus bohemians—his new environment offers every promise of fulfilment and a sense of belonging. However logical such expectations might be, they are nevertheless futile: placed in what appears to be his element, Kreisler not only fails to overcome his frustrations, but he grows to suffer from them more and more acutely, in an escalation of negative emotions which leads to increasingly violent outbursts, ending in rape, murder, and, ultimately, suicide.

What happens in Paris can therefore be seen as a process of turning a weak and frustrated individual into an embodiment of irrational and instinctive aggression, a phenomenon which Lewis seems particularly interested in exploring. Nine months after his arrival, Kreisler's situation is far from enviable: supplanted in Volker's favour by a more skilful borrower, a Russian-Pole named Louis Soltyk, he experiences his greatest financial strain ever. His usual sources of money have dried up and he has to salvage himself from landlords and creditors by changing his address. Having earned the reputation of a person who does not honour his obligations he cannot ask for more loans; with the exception of an

---

66   In this respect, Kreisler resembles Verloc who also expects financial gratification for what is, essentially, passivity and indolence. The fact that both protagonists meet a tragic end symbolically signifies a change in values taking place in modern society where wastrels are no longer indiscriminately accepted.

old leather suitcase he has nothing left to pawn, either. When we first encounter him in the novel, he is sitting in a room resembling a "funeral vault" (*T* 77) and waiting, against all odds, for a cheque from Kreisler Senior that is eight days overdue. Depression creeps up on him, and the prospect of suicide, hitherto invoked in letters to his father as a form of emotional blackmail, suddenly becomes very real: "How near was the end? This might be the end" (*T* 81). His instinct of self-preservation urges him to attempt more and more drastic means of acquiring funds, one of them being an amorous attachment to a prosperous woman who has just arrived in Paris and has not had a chance to hear about his debts and troubled past.

Kreisler's financial problems are thus inextricably linked with his turbulent love-life: a fatal combination whose destructive potential he almost seems to recognise in his determined pursuit of Anastasya Vasek. "A gold crown, regal person" fallen on "the wide shallow gap left by Ernst" (*T* 107), Anastasya becomes Kreisler's last vestige of hope: a god-sent opportunity to solve his predicament. Since his survival is at stake, some mechanistic will awakens in him and he sets out in indefatigable pursuit of his goal:

> He would respond to the utmost of his weakened ability; with certainty of failure, egoistically, but not at a standstill. Kreisler was a German, who by all rights and rules of national temperament, should have committed suicide some weeks earlier. Anastasya became an idée fixe. He was a machine, dead weight of old iron, that started, must go dashing on. (*T* 107)

Unfortunately, Kreisler's inability to find a niche for himself in the Parisian community is not only a question of insufficient funds. In order to win the woman of his dreams he must attend the ball at the Bonnington Club, and for this he needs his frac that has been pawned. The clothes which remain out of his reach symbolically underscore the hopelessness of his position: it is because of them that—as we read in the title that introduces him into the narrative—he is "doomed, evidently" (*T* 75). They stand for the superficial refinement necessary to affirm one's place in polite society: polished manners, moneyed ease and other graces that Kreisler does not possess. In Tarr's comedy of masks and roles, he becomes the only actor without a costume, and the pathos of his deprivation is amplified by the fact that he plays his part badly.

All in order for unbounded inflammation

However prominent throughout the plot of the novel, Kreisler's deprivation and frustration function only as a background against which Lewis skilfully constructs his portrayal of violence. Rather than emphasise what is a rather obvious psychological truth—frustration and deprivation *do* lead to violent outbursts—he attempts to trace the stages of this process, concentrating on how tensions grow in parallel with the decline of rational thinking. A lot of *Tarr* is devoted to a detailed analysis of an individual's ripening to violence, a transformation in which reason loses out against irrational imaginings. Kreisler's departure from rationalism is highlighted by his attitude towards Soltyk, who will gradually come to bear the fullest impact of the bewildered German's aggression.

The emergence of Soltyk as a scapegoat begins with his unintended victory in the competition for Volker's pocket—one of the first occasions when Kreisler's social skills are tested. Kreisler thus loses his patron to a rival who is "as empty and unsatisfactory as himself" (*T* 90) but who has a more effective method of "selling" his wastrelism:

> [Louis Soltyk] had superseded Kreisler in the position of influence as regards Volker's purse. Soltyk did not borrow a hundred marks. His system was far more up to date. = Ernst had experienced an unpleasant shock in coming into contact with Kreisler's slovenly and clumsy money habits again. (*T* 90)

Since both Kreisler and Soltyk are unproductive loafers and scroungers, their place in the pecking order depends solely on the style in which they try to manipulate others. In a socio-political reading of the above passage, Fredric Jameson sees the difference between the two protagonists in terms of "the shock between lower and higher cultures,"[67] where Kreisler is a throwback to some previous stage in the history of civilised conduct. Contrasted with Soltyk's "hereditary polish of manner" (*T* 138), Kreisler's awkwardness is barbaric: his machinations lack pretence and subtlety, his motives are too transparent for polite tastes. As he himself realises when a sudden attack of panic seizes him during his first conversation with Anastasya, he is "unaccustomed to act with calculation" (*T* 103) and this prevents him from making a good impression on others. In the over-refined company of bourgeois-bohemians, he sticks out as an incompatible individual, unable to play by society's rules and therefore running the risk of humiliation and rejection.

Meanwhile, the socially gifted Soltyk emerges from the narrative as Kreisler's "monstrous double"—it is in relation to him that the failing Prussian will define his position in the new environment. The two men are bound by a "mysterious and vexing kinship" (*T* 90) from which their rivalry naturally stems, as their similarity makes them aspire to the same social space and desire the same things. The likeness of their physical appearance additionally emphasises their status of enemy twins:

> Soltyk physically bore, distantly and with polish, a resemblance to Kreisler. His handsome face and elegance were very different. Kreisler and he disliked each other for obscure

---

67   Jameson, *Fables of Aggression: Wyndham Lewis*, 48.

physiological reasons: they had perhaps scrapped in the dressing room of Creation for some particularly fleshly covering, and each secured only fragments of a coveted garment. (*T* 90)

In the conflict for which they seem to have been programmed long before they actually meet, Soltyk happens to be the side privileged by fate. He represents, as Jameson rightly points out, "some more prosperous and well-favoured branch of the family, some far more successful second version, which can but reinforce the envy and resentment of the botched first draft."[68] Quite inconsiderately, rather than try to alleviate Kreisler's negative feelings towards him, Soltyk flaunts his superior position by speaking of his rival disparagingly or by belittling him in front of Volker:

> In an access of sentiment Ernst asked his new friend to try and sell a painting of Kreisler's. Soltyk dealt in paintings and art-objects. But Soltyk took him by the lapel of the coat and in a few words steadied him into cold sense.
> "Non! Sois pas bête! Here," he pulled out a handful of money and chose a dollar piece. "Here—give him this. You buy a *picture*—if it's a picture you want to buy—of Krashunine's. Kreisler has nothing but *Kreisler* to offer. C'est peu!" (*T* 90).

Unfortunately, Kreisler is more formidable than Soltyk expects and will not let such insults pass without retribution; he is only waiting for a sufficient pretext to release his pent-up anger. Things begin to go wrong when he discovers Soltyk's association with Anastasya, catching sight of them together at the Café Berne, after he has spent a whole day trying to pawn enough to redeem his frac. Overwhelmed by feelings of persecution and jealousy, he imagines that the Pole wants to interfere with his amorous plans by blackening his name, or even by usurping the woman of his dreams:

> Anastasya now provided him with an acceptable platform from which his vexation might spring at Soltyk. There was no money or insignificant male liaison to stuff him down into grumpiness. "Das Weib" was there. All was in order for unbounded inflammation. . . . What was [Soltyk] saying to her now? Sneers and ridicule, oceans of sneers directed at himself, more than ten thousand men could have discharged, he felt certainly were inundating

---

68   Jameson, *Fables of Aggression: Wyndham Lewis*, 92. Continuing his argument, Jameson reads the difference between Kreisler and Soltyk in the context of historical animosities between Germany and Poland: "In cultural terms, Kreisler's fury reenacts the humiliation of Germany, not merely before the more sophisticated culture of the West, but even in the face of the Frenchified and Westernised culture of subject Poland as well."

her ear. His stepmother fiancée, other tales, were being retailed. *Everything* that would

> her ear. His stepmother fiancée, other tales, were being retailed. *Everything* that would
> conceivably prejudice Anastasya, or would not, he accepted as already retailed. (*T* 121)

Whether Soltyk does indeed spread malicious stories is of little importance here; in fact Kreisler never bothers to verify his suspicions. He has found a convenient scapegoat onto whom all his frustrations—present and past, economical and sexual—can be projected. In Kreisler's eyes, Soltyk's guilt is twofold, parallel both with that of Kreisler's stepmother and of Kreisler's father: like the ex-fiancée, the Pole cuts Kreisler off from a source of income ("Behind Ernst and his parent Soltyk and his stepmother stood," *T* 121), and like Kreisler Senior, he complicates Kreisler's relationships with women. Acting an honourable Prussian nobleman, Kreisler considers it more appropriate to challenge Soltyk over "Das Weib" rather than money, but his real motive is the desire for "unbounded inflammation"—a discharge of the negative energy simmering inside him. He begins contemplating a violent assault on Soltyk, but would like to place it within a socially acceptable framework, so that his potential actions acquire a "moral" sanction. Reluctant to admit his contemptible impulses even to himself, he intuitively clings to an excuse which puts him in the most favourable light: hostile intent becomes attributed to others while he assumes the role of the offended party.

Soltyk, for his part, remains completely unaware that Kreisler obsessively collects "evidence" of his transgressions; he probably does not even know that Anastasya is a potential object of the Prussian's advances. The woman has hired him to act as her impresario, and therefore they are linked by "something equivalent to pleasant business relations" (*T* 150). She too fails to understand the cause of Kreisler's indignation when he spots her with Soltyk at Café Berne—it certainly does not occur to her that her business meeting might be interpreted as an act of betrayal by a man to whom she has spoken only once in her life. In general, Kreisler's Parisian acquaintances are oblivious to the turbulent emotions germinating within him; despite his increasingly extraordinary conduct (anti-social gestures, following people in the streets, aborted attempts at conversation, pretended self-absorption) nobody takes any interest in his insignificant person. He is left alone to cultivate his innumerable grudges and pretensions, gather new clues about the various schemes supposedly directed against him and become increasingly entrapped in spirals of twisted logic.

A sense of being constantly victimised by Soltyk is but an extreme example of Kreisler's general tendency to see in every action of others a reference to himself. To diagnose his condition, Lewis uses the term "persecution mania" (*T* 121), borrowed from psychiatric discourse and suggesting a pathological distortion of reality.[69] Although Kreisler is not a

---

69   Some critics see this as an invitation to view Kreisler as a pathological case (this is a valid
     interpretative choice, though one which excludes the possibility of any normative analysis of
     his behaviour). David Trotter, for example, goes so far as to read the whole of *Tarr* as a study

patient in a lunatic asylum but a self-conscious young man pushed to the limit of endurance by his accumulating misfortunes, the tortuous workings of his mind are frequently a muddle of hallucinations concerning other people and their intentions. He feels he is the target of his friends' ridicule (*T* 92) and "a victim of strategy" (*T* 90) among the ladies of the Lipmann circle, imagines that Anastasya purposefully makes him embarrassed (*T* 105), suspects the customers at the Restaurant Lejeune of eavesdropping on his conversations (*T* 105), and believes that Volker snubs him in the street (*T* 115). His touchiness receives the most comic articulation in the brilliant scene when he meets the Englishman Lowndes and contemplates asking him for a loan. Too shy to make the request straight away, he wastes his time on various strategic manoeuvres to soften his potential creditor but in the end fails to say what he wants. Throughout the conversation, he has the impression that Lowndes stubbornly avoids touching on the problem of money and that his obliviousness is only a ruse: "The nearness they had been to this demand must have affected, he thought, even his impervious companion. He *had* asked and been refused, to all intents and purposes" (*T* 115).

Kreisler's twisted reasoning can thus be seen to reveal an important aspect of Lewis's reflection on violence: the observation that a heightening of aggression is invariably accompanied by a departure from rational thinking. Naming an enemy and charging him with an imaginary insult justifies for Kreisler the necessity for revenge, allows him to cultivate his aggressive impulses, and puts him on a path towards violence. With his mental state dangerously bordering on paranoia, he becomes less and less resistant to anger, however irrational and ill-justified it might be: the "unbounded inflammation" is now only a matter of time.

A thirst for action

Stretched over two chapters, the ball episode is a turning point in Kreisler's relationship with the Parisian community in that it puts a definitive end to his hopes of assimilation and marks his transformation into an enemy figure, set over against the world which rejects him. It is the moment when Kreisler, dressed in an inappropriate set of clothes, decides to confront Soltyk and the entire Lipmann coterie. The resolution to appear at a formal ball despite his shabby attire can be seen as an act of desperation, a neurotic attempt to gain certainty about his position. At the same time, there is a touch of barbarism about it: the prospect of violating the bourgeois-bohemian dress code strikes Kreisler as appealing, to the extent that he deliberately dirties his jacket by rubbing it against a whitewashed wall.

---

of paranoia, and detects aberrant mental states in both of the novel's main protagonists. See: David Trotter, *Paranoid Modernism: Literary Experiment, Psychosis and the Professionalization of English Society,* (Oxford: Oxford University Press, 2001).

This gesture, qualifying as both aggressive and auto-aggressive, indicates the direction in which Kreisler's behaviour will evolve. Slouching towards Fräulein Lipmann's salon to be born is a rough beast—the New, envisaged as "the rampant male, split at the core, a destroyer fuelled by his own self-destruction,"[70] that, according to Dennis Brown, foreshadows the dramatic fall of the whole pre-World War I social order.

Guarding himself against the mortifications he will have to suffer, Kreisler assumes the pose of an invader, going on a sortie into enemy territory. Lewis describes his activities in militarist language, resonant with the belligerent atmosphere that characterised the times of *Tarr*'s composition. Thus, Kreisler arriving at Fräulein Lipmann's door announces himself with "a hoarse Z-like blast" of the bell (*T* 129), and once he gets inside, he indulges in strategic planning, observing the movements of the guests in the room, deciding to "mark time . . . until the opportunity arrive[s] to strike" (*T* 138) but constantly forgetting that he has "made his position untenable" (*T* 138) by his extravagant clothes and conduct. On the way to the dance he holds Bertha Lunken "as hostage," (*T* 145) implicating her in his manoeuvres, and as the party enters the Bonnington Club, he establishes "his headquarters" (*T* 151) in the conservatory, from where he ventures on "tours of inspection," evoking "an expectant or anxious tremor" (*T* 152) among the society ladies. Finally, as his disastrous mission draws to a close, he becomes "the old Berserker warrior, ravening and irresistible" (*T* 157)—a comparison which again emphasises Kreisler's barbaric nature, equalling him to a villain of the Viking sagas.[71]

The concentration of militarist expressions is not accidental: it indicates another stage in Kreisler's progression towards unhinged violence. His emotions are no longer merely troubling him; he is now ready to let them rule:

[Kreisler's] endless dissatisfaction and depression could only be satisfied by *active* things, unlike *itself*. Soltyk's self-possessed and masterly signs of distinguished camaraderie

---

70   Brown, *Intertextual Dynamics*, 68.

71   In the context of Kreisler's behaviour throughout the ball scene—his inappropriate dress, his inclination to drink and the way in which he works himself up to the point of hysteria—Lewis's comparison of him to a Berserker warrior seems particularly apt. *Cf.* a definition of a Berserker warrior: "The word berserker comes from two Norse words *bjørn* meaning *bear* or *bare* (naked) and *serkr* meaning *shirt*, a reference to the fact that a berserker warrior went into battle dressed in bear skins or without any armour at all. Berserkers thought that by wearing the fur of the bear, they would become possessed by the animal's spirit and would gain its strength—a way of shape-shift into the animal's form. Shape-shifting was important as their pagan gods also had this ability. The meaning of the word berserker is derived from another characteristic of this warrior—*berserkergang*—a word meaning crazed behaviour. Before a battle, berserkers spent hours working themselves into a frenzy by painting their faces, howling like animals, banging helmets, consuming large quantities of alcohol or eating hallucinogenic mushrooms." *Viking warriors. The Berserker.* The Viking History Theme Page. Retrieved 1st December, 2003. < http://www.stemnet.nf.ca/CITE/v_berserker.htm >

depressed Kreisler very much. The Russian *had been there once* at the critical moment, and was, more distantly, an attribute of Volker. He did not like him. = How it would satisfy him to dig his fingers into that flesh and tear it like thick cloth! = He was "for it": he was going out. He was being helped off by things. = Why did he not *shout*? He longed to *act*: the rusty machine had a thirst for action. His energies were repudiating their master. (*T* 150)

Accordingly, the ball scene is where Kreisler's first, chaotic outbursts of aggression take place. His attacks on accidental victims and surges of violent energy followed by inertia clearly anticipate a more focused assault in which his pent-up hatred of anyone he has come into contact with will make him want to destroy them.

Kreisler's disruptive behaviour at the ball quickly becomes noticed by his bourgeois-bohemian audience, who sense "something unusual in his presence besides his dress and the disorder even of that" (*T* 132). As an awkward liar spreading falsehoods that are immediately found out, a buffoon speaking "with ingenious circumlocutions . . . in a dialect calculated to bewilder the most acute psychologist" (*T* 147), a bad dancer "stamping a little bit as though he mistook the waltz for a more primitive music" (*T* 148), and a lecher causing young girls to leave his company "with scarlet faces" (*T* 150), he grabs the attention of everybody in the ballroom. Yet, for most of the evening, he is not treated very seriously; unaware of his militant mood, people suspect he simply has had too much drink and try to avoid him.

In his unbalanced state of mind, this reaction wounds Kreisler deeply, especially as he himself has great difficulty in sustaining his enemy role. Despite the aura of aggression he is attempting to create, he remains vulnerable: the soft voice of Anastasya can "unman" him within seconds (*T* 134), the fact that Soltyk snubs him draws him to the point of hysteria, his embarrassment at not being dressed for the occasion makes him compulsively talk about "the stately edifice in the Rue de Rennes" (*T* 147) which keeps his frac. Once more, Kreisler is betrayed by the part he has chosen—the drama does not go as planned and, rather than work towards the destruction of others, he mainly destroys himself with his obsessive thoughts:

Reality was so much more complicated than Kreisler's forecast of it. All was passing so differently. Soltyk showed interest in nothing in the world but his discussion with some man in a corner. Yet he was the obvious object to carry off some of Kreisler's wrath, and seemed deliberately disappointing him. All these people allied with and privy to Fate, acted in an unexpected and maliciously natural way. There was a plot to deny his fermentations. = His were the sensations of a simple man introduced for the first time into an official milieu,—a court or courthouse—where everybody, behaving strangely, seems quite at home and born to it all. The propriety and good sense of all these people! He was the only one not in Fate's secrets. (*T* 138-139)

Characteristically for Kreisler, his choice to oppose everyone flips over into a sense that everyone is against him. Anticipating rejection, he exploits it even before it has taken place, for example by deciding at the outset of the Lipmann party that "he felt . . . a sort of outcast. . . . He did not become timid and deprecatory, but a haughty and insurgent outcast" (*T* 139).

Like many modernist protagonists, Kreisler alternates between the roles of victim and victimiser (though his claim to being the former is probably lesser than that of, say, Winnie Verloc). His aggression stems from a feeling of resentment at the way the world treats him, regardless of whether this unfair treatment is real or imagined. The ball scene well illustrates this tendency, showing Kreisler vacillate between bouts of self-pity and covert rage, both poles of his psychological trajectory gaining in intensity as the evening progresses. The sight of Anastasya, for instance, induces in him the following chain of emotions: at first he is smitten by her beauty, but instantly recalls "the suicide of his dreams" (*T* 133) that she has caused and frowns at her, only to plant a most devoted kiss on her hand a second later. When she reappears before him accompanied by Soltyk, he wishes to "insult her," "bare her soul," and "spit on it" (*T* 152) but lapses into depression again when, having attracted her attention, he receives a derisory smile. Following a sinusoidal pattern, Kreisler's reactions move from a desire to "strike [Anastasya] in the mouth" (*T* 154) and to "possess her" violently (*T* 157), down to feeling "like a martyr" (*T* 158), publicly humiliated by his unattainable beloved. A similar emotional confusion manifests itself in Kreisler's relations with other people: Soltyk, Bertha, and, later in the novel, also with Tarr. From the evening of the party onwards, the "recoil and flow of anger"[72] become the key dynamics governing Kreisler's behaviour, punctuating his life with outbursts of willed self-assertion and spells of apathy, which propel him inevitably towards a tragic end.

Trapped by his self-destructive psychology, Kreisler turns into a figure of passionate excess, completely unpredictable and prone to abrupt losses of control. The energy simmering within him is bound for entropic release; it cannot be put to constructive use but must exhaust itself in random surges, fits of violent abandon that mark his passage through the plot. This dangerous potential is first revealed in a series of dance floor incidents at the Bonnington Club when Kreisler, careening round the room with Mrs Bevelage, throws the whole party into chaos. In a symbolic scene, he and his disorientated partner assume the form of a missile, about to burst outside and glide through the city, but miraculously diverted from its course at the last moment:

> He took her twice, with ever-increasing velocity, round the large hall, and at the third round, at breakneck speed, spun with her in the direction of the front door. . . . Another

---

72   Brown, *Intertextual Dynamics*, 68.

moment and they would have been in the street, amongst the traffic, a disturbing
meteor, whizzing out of sight, had they not met the alarmed resistance of a considerable
English family entering the front door as Kreisler bore down upon it. (*T* 148)

Not unlike Conrad's Professor among the metropolitan crowd, Kreisler surrounded
by a swarm of dancers is an "enemy within," a human explosive ready to go off at the
slightest pretext. Overwhelmed by the sight of "trunkless, living heads rolling and
bobbing past, a sea of them"[73] (*T* 152), he is burning with misanthropic hatred for which
he badly needs to find an outlet. Ideally, he would vent his fury on Soltyk, who offers "a
conventional target for violence" (*T* 152), but the Russian-Pole is nowhere to be found.
Feeling increasingly exasperated, Kreisler must content himself with random victims:
his aggression is first channelled towards a shy man dancing with Anastasya, and then
towards Fräulein Lipmann and other unsuspecting females. Poor Mrs Bevelage is swept
off to the dance floor again, this time to be used as a battering ram and brought to the
ground in humiliation:

> Their hostess also was dancing. Kreisler noted her with a wink of recognition. = Dancing
> very slowly, almost mournfully, he and his partner bumped into her each time as they
> passed. The widow felt the impact, but it was only at the third round that she perceived
> the method and intention inducing these bumps. The collision could not be avoided. . . .
> At the fourth turn of the room, however, Kreisler having increased her speed sensibly,
> she was on her guard, and in fact already suggesting that she should be taken to her
> seat. He pretended to be giving their hostess a wide berth this time, but suddenly and
> gently swerved, and bore down upon her. The widow veered frantically, took a false step,
> tripped on her dress, tearing it, and fell to the ground.—They caused a circular undulating
> commotion through the neighbouring dancers, like a stone falling in a pond. (*T* 155-156)

Bumping into people is for Kreisler a form of energetic discharge, an early version
of the pogo—a dance for the socially incompatible. It reduces him to a "wild body,"
reminiscent of the primitive protagonists of Lewis's short fiction[74] who are little more than
lumps of brute matter, enslaved to their instincts. Like them, Kreisler seeks immediate
gratification; his actions, including those violent ones, are not linked to any long-term
goal but rely on impulse. (In this respect he differs from the Professor of *The Secret
Agent* whose whole life is determined by an *idée fixe*—the quest for the ideal detonator.)

---

73   Kreisler's paranoid vision parallels those of the Professor in *The Secret Agent*: he too positions
     himself outside the multitude, finding their actions alien and incomprehensible.

74   See: Wyndham Lewis, *The Complete Wild Body*, Bernard Lafourcade, ed., (Santa Barbara:
     Black Sparrow Press, 1982).

"A creature of whim without any self-wisdom,"[75] Kreisler begets chaos purposelessly, on the spur of a moment, with no attempt at justifying his antics: "He merely went on farcing because he could think of nothing else to do" (*T* 156). His anger disrupts his integrity, making him incapable of coherent response and eventually subverting his performance. Those he would really like to abuse, Anastasya and Soltyk, have no idea about his intentions; despite all the murderous thoughts, Kreisler has failed to provoke a confrontation. The events of the evening fill him with a sense of uncertainty and disappointment: "This should have been a climax, of blows, words, definite things. But things remained vague" (*T* 159). The one certainty he does have is that he must act—his progression towards violence has reached a point of no return.

She had lain in wait for him

When at the ball Kreisler crosses the threshold of violence, he does so by using his body as a social-sexual weapon while taking out his frustrations on unsuspecting females. For Lewis, there seems to be a noticeable connection between aggression and sexuality: the plot of *Tarr* provides a number of occasions where the interdependence of the two is highlighted and explored. What transpires in the course of the novel is that violence may well have sexual overtones, and the gradual progression towards the former is mirrored by increasingly aggressive acts characterised by the latter.

Accordingly, after his relatively innocent antics, as his manic dances at the ball may be termed, Kreisler's next transgression is far more serious, and—significantly—again directed against a victim who is not likely to retaliate or demand retribution. Bertha Lunken, vulnerable after a recent break-up with Tarr, falls easy prey to Kreisler's bullying masculinity, prostrating herself in his path exactly at the moment when everybody else has chosen to avoid him. They are first thrown together on their way to the Bonnington Club when, in a fit of romantic fancy, Bertha offers affection to her brooding compatriot and magnanimously allows him to kiss and embrace her. Her sudden sentiment is obviously alloyed by a less noble impulse to get at Tarr: knowing that rumours circulate fast in the Parisian community, she wants "to be seen with Kreisler" (*T* 184), but hopes that "with the salt of jealousy and a really big row" (*T* 143) her ex-fiancée can be won back. Too preoccupied with her feminine tricks to recognise the hazards of the situation, Bertha continues her flirtation with Kreisler after the ball, turning a blind eye to the scandal he has caused there, and ignoring both the warnings of the Lipmann circle and the voice of her intuition. In a symbolic scene when her new admirer pays her a visit for the first time, she has a premonition of her living-space being intruded upon but does nothing to avert the threat: "it was *he*, the enemy getting

---

75   Brown, *Intertextual Dynamics*, 68.

in. She wished to stop him there, before he came any further" (*T* 185). Instead, she clings to the role she has chosen to play before the bourgeois-bohemian world—that of a self-sacrificing altruist, supporting her artist friend at a critical juncture of his life. Like every performance in *Tarr*, this one too must go horribly wrong: in trying to use Kreisler for her own purposes, Bertha gets more than she has bargained for and is raped, thus ironically acquiring the martyr status she has been pretending to have.

For Kreisler, the assault on Bertha is little more than satisfying an "appetite," just as the kiss on the way to the dance is a negligible episode "to embellish his programme" (*T* 142). It almost seems that he abuses her willy-nilly, simply because she gives him an opportunity to do so:

> He was under the impression, however, that she had lain in wait for him. He was so accustomed to think of her in that character! If she had been in full flight he would have imagined that she was only decoying him. She was a woman who could not help adhering. (*T* 178)

No complex argumentation is summoned in order to rationalise the use of violence against Bertha; sensing her naivety and accessibility, Kreisler feels entitled to take advantage of her. She is "rapeable" exactly in the way in which "a murderee is murderable" for Rupert Birkin in *Women in Love*: her persecutor shifts the responsibility onto her, believing that she subconsciously desires to be victimised. After her body has been exploited, she is sent away "as a workman would have been, who had been there to mend a shutter or rectify a bolt" (*T* 195). Kreisler does not experience any moral misgivings; on the contrary, he has to feign an apology when within thirty minutes from the incident he comes "to see his victim" (*T* 200). Rather than seek Bertha's pardon, he wants to secure the possibility of future transgressions: his visit is motivated by "an intuition not to lose her absolutely, the wisdom of his appetite counselling" (*T* 200).

As a representative of patriarchal culture, Kreisler is quite confident that he will get away with his abominable deed (the thought that someone may learn about it crosses his mind only once, during a conversation with Tarr, but even then he feels no remorse or fear). He can boast a long history of dishonourable conduct towards women for which he has never had to bear any responsibility: despite frequent amorous adventures and a considerable number of illegitimate children, he has kept clear of any commitments and resisted the roles of husband and father. He operates on the assumption that women exist in order to serve male needs—they are a "vast dumping-ground for sorrow and affliction," "a world-dimensioned Pawn-shop," in which a man can deposit himself whenever he is "in straits" (*T* 101). The text identifies Kreisler as someone who "approached a love affair as a Korps-student engages in a student's duel," "stoically certain that blood would be drawn" (*T* 102). Violence is implicit in his perception of gender roles; he is exposed as a bully who scapegoats females for his own failures:

> Much might be noticed in common between him and the drunken navvy on a Saturday night who comes home bellicosely towards his wife, blows raining gladly at the mere sight of her. He may get practically all the excitement and exertion he violently needs, without any of the sinister chances a more real encounter would present. His wife is "his little bit" of unreality, or play. He can declaim, be outrageous to the top of his bent; can be maudlin, too; all conducted almost as he pleases, with none of the shocks of the real and too tragic world. (*T* 102)

The assault on Bertha is a logical consequence of this attitude. Because in "the real and too tragic world" Kreisler has met Anastasya (the novel's embodiment of a "new woman") who intimidates him and who completely ignores his advances, he must project his anger onto another object, someone whom he considers a subordinate being. Rape becomes a way of asserting his male domination, an attempt to defend the traditional power structures that Anastasya has undermined: primeval sexual instincts begin to fuel the desire for a violent release of accumulated tension.

The bubonic plague

At one point in the novel, Tarr pesters Bertha with the question: "What, after all, does *Kreisler* mean?," but receives only a cursory answer, "as though Kreisler were the bubonic plague and she were making light of it" (*T* 227). In his insightful reading of Lewis's text, Michael Levenson proposes that human interaction is portrayed in it as a kind of infection: character traits are passed over from one individual to another and the boundaries of identity are obliterated.[76] "All personality [is] catching," as Tarr observes, and people are "sicknesses for each other" (*T* 72). In Kreisler's case, only a comparison to an epidemic properly renders his effect on the Parisian community, since nearly everybody who comes into contact with him is inevitably drawn into a maelstrom of trouble.

The spreading of aggression is an important aspect in Lewis's analysis, and one which the novel carefully foregrounds. As the plot develops, it becomes obvious that Kreisler begets chaos in the life of the main protagonists: Soltyk's—whom he steamrolls into a farcical duel, Bertha's—whom he rapes and impregnates, Tarr's and Anastasya's— because they both bear the consequences of his unfortunate fatherhood. Minor figures,

---

76   Michael Levenson, *Modernism and the Fate of Individuality*, 136-137. Drawing on Levenson's reflections, the present reading will complement them with a discussion of masculine aggressiveness, also construed in *Tarr* as contagious.

such as Fräulein Lipmann, Ernst Volker, Lowndes, Mrs Bevelage, Soltyk's seconds, and even the staff of the police station in which Kreisler hangs himself, are all negatively affected by his disruptive presence and implicated in his fate. As Lewis once suggested in a jocular plot synopsis of *Tarr*, the whole book is about "the elaborate and violent form of suicide selected by Herr Kreisler, involving a number of other people."[77]

Yet Kreisler is a plague also in another sense: he brings violence into the bourgeois-bohemian world and makes it spread like an infectious disease. Under his influence other males in the novel begin to display aggressive tendencies, either because they want to confront the quarrelsome Prussian as rivals (Tarr, Soltyk) or because they take sides in his conflict with somebody else (Bitzenko, Staretsky, Khudin). With his explosive temperament, Kreisler serves as a catalyst for evil instincts dormant in the Parisian community: he stirs bad blood, introduces tension, and provokes his opponents beyond endurance. The spite that emanates from him is mirrored by those who surround him, and multiplied through reciprocal escalation. When the pressure of pent-up emotions grows unbearable, the possibility of a cathartic bloodletting begins to seem an attractive option, even to the characters initially opposed to the idea of solving conflicts by force. In the light of anthropological theory, contagion with violence occurs through mimesis: an act of hostility is likely to incite a similar reaction.[78] Lewis's angry males invariably follow this pattern, letting themselves be pulled into a maze of hatred and abuse. The chaos of the duel scene, during which all involved leap at each other's throats with violent abandon, is a logical consequence of their interaction with Kreisler, as well as the ultimate proof of their corruption.

One of the first protagonists to catch the germ of violence is Tarr—the figure who seems the least corruptible and is frequently taken to be the novel's centre of moral discrimination, or even Lewis's spokesman.[79] Many critics see him and Kreisler as antithetical types, representing the true artist and the false, the mind and the body, contemplation and reckless action, restraint and indulgence, rationality and emotion, or ego and id. In these binary schemes Tarr occupies the positive pole: he is associated with values which facilitate the control of aggressive impulses, and which Western culture considers supportive of civilization and order.[80] As a believer

---

77   Wyndham Lewis, *Rude Assignment*, (London: Hutchinson, 1950), 151.

78   Girard, *Violence and the Sacred*, 26-27.

79   See for example: Materer, *Wyndham Lewis, the Novelist*, (Detroit: Wayne State University Press, 1976), 57.

80   As Barbara Whitmer maintains, Western culture poses violence in opposition to rationality, relating it to the sphere of emotions or biological necessities (violence is seen as endemic to the human species). The mind becomes privileged because it is thought to be capable of transcending violent impulses. See: Whitmer, *The Violence Mythos*, 12-13.

in the supremacy of the intellect, who aspires to evolve beyond human weakness, Tarr is probably the only character in the novel likely to invite the reader's trust. Yet as Michael Levenson rightly points out, Lewis departs from a familiar modernist paradigm where the contemplative individual functions as a supreme arbiter, capable of sifting the meaning of events.[81] Although the reader may expect that Tarr, like Conrad's Marlow in *Heart of Darkness*, will cast a critical eye on other characters' depravity, he actually yields to Kreisler's provocation, is drawn into a conflict, and only thanks to an unexpected substitution avoids a violent confrontation.

Tarr's contamination with violence begins with his involvement in a love triangle intrigue conceived by Bertha. It is at this point that he and Kreisler are first brought together as successive lovers of the same woman and immediately develop a mutual dislike, although their relations bear every appearance of politeness and cordiality. Despite his professed willingness to free himself from the shackles of lust, Tarr cannot help being jealous with regard to his ex-fiancée: the prospect of a rival reawakens his interest in her so that he resembles "a man who hears that the rind of the fruit he has just been eating is good, and comes back to his plate to devour the part he has discarded" (*T* 220). Irritated by the "air of proprietorship" (*T* 217) which Tarr displays towards Bertha, Kreisler immediately grows more possessive of his prey, even though he has no serious plans regarding her. In this way both men get trapped in a cycle of mimetic desire, where the attractiveness of the pursued object depends largely on whether someone else competes for it.[82] Bertha's person, for whom neither Tarr nor Kreisler would care much if nobody stood in their way, suddenly becomes important to them, although not as an end in itself, but as a means of proving their superiority over their rival. What counts in this game is not being with Bertha but preventing the other suitor from being with her—she is just a pretext for a masculine power struggle[83] which, once begun, quickly escalates to dangerous proportions.

Ousted from the position of dominance, Tarr must take the initiative in the developing conflict, or disappear from Bertha and Kreisler's life. Reason advises him to do the latter, but the process of contagion is already underway and an urge to confront his successor prevails. He follows Kreisler every night to various bohemian haunts and begins to socialise with him, ostensibly to cure himself of his nostalgia for his lost relationship:

---

81   Levenson, *Modernism and the Fate of Individuality*, 139.

82   See Chapter I of this study, section: "Mimetic Rivalries and Contagion of Violence," 19-21.

83   Both Tarr and Kreisler are guilty of reification in their treatment of Bertha. She is perceived as property over which "territoral' wars can be fought: Tarr thinks of her body as of "premises" that his rival has "taken possession of" (*T* 216), and Kreisler gets ready to assert his newly-established ownership rights: "If the Englishman's amiability were a polite way of reclaiming property left ownerless and therefore susceptible of new rights being created, then in time those *later* rights would be vindicated" (*T* 217).

The causes at the root of Tarr's present thrusting of himself upon Kreisler were the same as his later visits at the Lipmann's. A sort of bath of Germans was his prescription for himself, a voluptuous immersion. To heighten the effect, he was being German himself; being Bertha as well. (*T* 221)

Tarr's self-prescribed therapy is, however, only a form of delusion. An exposure to German influence causes him to open himself to the drives and desires he has hitherto tried to suppress. If, as Fredric Jameson claims, the Germans of *Tarr* represent the forces of the id[84] (Kreisler—aggression, Bertha—sexuality), then Tarr's increasing "Germanness" symbolically underscores his transition to a different mode of functioning. Under the guise of a nostalgic purgation, he sets out in pursuit of primitive satisfaction, gradually transforming from an ascetic intellectual into an angry, jealous male. Every meeting with Kreisler draws him further and further away from his contemplative ideal: the more he engages in his petty sexual dramas, the less time he spends in the studio. His ambitions no longer lie in creative work, but centre around questions of power (becoming an "interferer and voluntary policeman" (*T* 227) for Kreisler), revenge (paying Bertha back for her "Kreisler stunt," *T* 227), and sexual accomplishment (seducing Anastasya). Before he knows it, he falls victim to what Michael Levenson terms "transitivity"[85]—the passing of personality features from one character to another—and comes to resemble not only Bertha, but even his own rival, Kreisler.

The change that Tarr undergoes remains in agreement with Girard's theory of mimetic triangles, according to which rivals coveting the same thing or person inevitably turn into mirror-images of each other. Ironically, the more similar they grow, the more different they perceive themselves to be: "the *sameness* with which they are obsessed appears to them as absolute *otherness*."[86] They judge their own desires and attitudes as autonomous and justified, while those of the rival—as irrational, aggressive and harmful.[87] Thus, Kreisler does not recognise Tarr's "Germanness" but is nevertheless irritated by his manner, and Tarr feels distinctly unlike Kreisler although he keeps imitating him. Each sees the other as an intruder and provoker, yet both pretend (as mimetic rivals often do) that the bone of their contention does not exist and that they are not interested in conflict at all. The dynamics governing their relationship (reciprocal mirroring, denial of the problem, attributing hostile intent to the rival) are visible even within the span of a short conversation such as this one:

---

84   Jameson, *Wyndham Lewis*, 89.

85   Levenson, *Modernism and the Fate of Individuality*, 135.

86   René Girard, *Deceit, Desire, and the Novel,* trans. Yvonne Freccero, (Baltimore: The Johns Hopkins Press, 1961), 106.

87   See Chapter I of this study, section: "Mimetic Rivalries and Contagion of Violence," 19-21.

"Have you seen Fräulein Lunken to-day?"

"No." As Tarr was coming to the point Kreisler condescended to speak: "I shall see her tomorrow morning."

A space for protest or comment seemed to be left after this sentence, in Kreisler's still very "speaking" expression.

Tarr smiled at the tone of this piece of information. Kreisler at once grinned, mockingly, in return.

"You can get out of your head any idea that I have turned up to interfere with your proceedings," Tarr then said. "Affairs lie entirely between Fräulein Lunken and yourself."

Kreisler met this assurance truculently.

"You could not interfere with my proceedings. I do what I want to do in this life!"

"How splendid. *Wunderbar*! I admire you!"

"Your admiration is not asked for!"

"It leaps up involuntarily! Prosit! But I did not mean, Herr Kreisler, that my desire to interfere, had such desire existed, would have been tolerated. Oh no! I meant that no such desire existing, we had no cause for quarrel. Prosit!"

Tarr again raised his glass expectantly and coaxingly, peering steadily at the German. He said, "Prosit" as he would have said, "Peeep-oh!"

"Pros't!" Kreisler answered with alarming suddenness, and an alarming diabolical smile. "Prosit!" with finality. He put his glass down. "That is all right. I have no *desire*," he wiped and struck up his moustaches, "to *quarrel* with anybody. I wish to be left alone. That is all."

"To be left alone to enjoy your friendship with Bertha—that is your meaning? Am I not right? I see."

"That is my business. I wish to be left *alone*."

"Of course it's your business, my dear chap. Have another drink!" (*T* 221-222)

By playing tit-for-tat endlessly, mimetic rivals enter a path towards violence from which it is virtually impossible to divert. Tarr senses this danger before his critical faculties are entirely gone and undertakes an attempt at liberating himself from the "three-legged affair" (*T* 229). As he intuits correctly, the introduction of a fourth party might "make things solid and less precarious again" (*T* 229), but unfortunately his choice falls on Anastasya—the object of Kreisler's unrequited passion. Instead of transforming the triangular structure into a rectangle, he produces two more, partly overlapping, triangles of desire (Tarr—Anastasya—Kreisler; Anastasya—Tarr—Bertha). The collision of interests is far more intense than before, especially as both Tarr and Kreisler value Anastasya much more highly than Bertha. As a potential recipient of Anastasya's affection, Tarr cannot escape Kreisler's resentment and thus finds himself drawn into conflict again:

Tarr began to scent another mysterious muddle. Would he never be free of Herr Kreisler? Perhaps he was going to be followed and rivalled in this too? With deliberate meditation Kreisler appeared to be coming round to Tarr's opinion. . . . Tarr felt inclined to say, "But you don't understand! She is for *me*. *Bertha* is your young lady now!" Only in reflecting on this possible remark, he was confronted with the obvious reply, "But *is* Bertha my young lady?" (*T* 231)

At this level of complication, the enmity between Tarr and Kreisler enters its final stage in which a radical confrontation seems unavoidable. Lewis gives us a foretaste of it when Tarr pays his rival a "bellicose visit" (*T* 247) and must beat a hasty retreat, threatened with a dog-whip. The incident is for him the last drop of poison, completing the process of his contamination: obsessed with the idea of revenge, he loses his grip on reality and begins to think like a paranoid. Soon, we see him reaching a state of nervous agitation comparable to that of Kreisler in the earlier scenes of the novel; the well-known scenario unfolds again, only re-enacted by a new figure. In the climactic section of the narrative Tarr, all braced for a definitive clash, cruises the cafés of Paris with the same violent frenzy that once sent Kreisler through the Bonnington Club in pursuit of Soltyk. On finding his rival in the company of a stranger, "completely wrapped up in some engrossing game or conspiracy" (*T* 248), he is as disappointed as Kreisler must have been when he was ignored by Soltyk at the ball. Although the circumstances are not favourable for a fight, there is no turning back for Tarr—he has become yet another of Lewis's "wild bodies," seeking energetic discharge. His mind conjures up a distorted vision of reality, in which he is a victim of Kreisler's intrigue and may be attacked at any moment.

A surprising recognition occurs when the blow that Tarr is waiting for falls on "another man snatched up into his role" (*T* 251)—the unfortunate Louis Soltyk. All the carefully constructed tension deflates in an instant, only to begin building up in a new configuration of relationships. As a result, Tarr is given a chance to recover from the plague: the mimetic process of violent escalation is suddenly brought to a halt. The fact that he has found himself outside the mainstream of events is obviously not easy to accept for the egocentric Englishman—his first impulse is to "[follow] Kreisler at once and [get] up a second row . . . punch Kreisler's head, fight about a little bit, and then depart, his business done" (*T* 251)—yet after a while a sobering reflection arrives. Irritation gives way to a feeling of relief that someone else plays Tarr's part while he is free to back out unobtrusively:

As [Tarr] watched the man Kreisler had struck, he seemed to be watching himself. And yet he felt rather on the side of Kreisler. With a mortified chuckle he prepared to pay for his drink and be off, leaving Kreisler for ever to his very complicated, mysterious and turbulent existence. (*T* 251)

In Girardian terms, Soltyk's function can be seen as that of a sacrificial victim that helps to re-route Tarr and Kreisler's violence against each other. It is onto him that both parties displace their need for revenge; the latent hostilities become symbolically assuaged through a seemingly unrelated act of aggression.[88] Challenged to a fight over Anastasya,[89] Soltyk pays for Tarr's sins and bears the full weight of Kreisler's wrath. Interestingly, although Tarr senses that an unfair substitution has occurred, his sentiment lies with the assailant rather than the recipient of the blows. (This is partly because Tarr's vanity is hurt by what he interprets as Kreisler's snub; Soltyk is in a way his rival when it comes to attracting Kreisler's attention.) A logical consequence of this is the truce which takes place between Tarr and Kreisler a little later when the former agrees to act as the latter's second in a duel with Soltyk (although only until a replacement can be found). Their antithetical positions are momentarily reconciled, and Tarr, steadied into cold sense by the violent scene he has witnessed, uses this opportunity to withdraw entirely from the affair.

Kreisler's attack on Soltyk opens the way for a whole series of new infections, especially as it is meant to be a prelude to a more profound clash, for which a number of participants are required. Aware of the fact that Soltyk might not be interested in a confrontation with him at all, Kreisler sets out to stage a duel, relying on culturally constructed methods of implicating people in violence. For his mission to be successful, he finds himself a henchman—the Russian Bitzenko, known in the bourgeois-bohemian world as a devotee of duelling—whom he wins over by giving him a false picture of his feud with Soltyk. Working in tandem, and using different methods of persuasion (Kreisler—insults and blows, Bitzenko—lofty talk about honour), they manage to drag Soltyk into a conflict he does not want to enter, over a matter that he does not quite understand. He, in turn, passes the germ of hatred and aggression onto his companions, Staretsky and Khudin, who consent to serve as his seconds. Since both the slapping

---

88   See Chapter I of this study, section: "Mimetic Rivalries and Contagion of Violence," 19-21.

89   Anastasya is the official reason why Kreisler turns on Soltyk, although, of course, there are many others (usurpation of Kreisler's social space, cutting Kreisler off from a source of income). An interesting question, as far as character psychology is concerned, is why Tarr gets away with his flirtation with Anastasya so easily. Kreisler knows that the two may be romantically involved (he sees them together in the street, just as he sees Anastasya with Soltyk—in terms of "evidence" Tarr's and Soltyk's guilt is the same), but all he chooses to do to Tarr is to issue a warning: "I saw you with another lady to-night. . . . Be careful I don't come and pull your nose when I see you with that other lady!" (*T* 239). It is possible that Kreisler underestimates Tarr as a rival, or that he considers Soltyk's guilt much more serious simply because he sees him as the first in the long row of potential usurpers (cf. the following fragment: "[Kreisler] had lived with [Anastasya] instinctively in this solitary world of he and she. It was quite changed at present. Soltyk had got into it. Soltyk, by implication, brought a host of others, even if he did not mean that he was a definite rival there himself." (*T* 121)).

of Soltyk and the duel negotiations take place in a café, all the people present at the scene—the garçons, the manager, the customers—are at risk of contagion with violence, through the passive observation of the spectacle unfolding before their eyes. In an anthropologically sensitive manner, Lewis notes the attractiveness of violence to the onlookers: the incident makes all conversations die down and "the entire Café appear[s] to be participating" (*T* 252).

Among the crowd of potential plague victims, Tarr is the only person who takes the opposite trajectory. His determination to leave and have nothing more to do with Kreisler holds the promise of recovery: he seems to have already realised that violence has a mesmerising power and therefore he does not want to be exposed to it any longer. Although he has been cast in the role of Kreisler's other second (beside Bitzenko), he remains silent throughout the negotiation sequence and departs as soon as the talking is over. On the other hand, he makes no attempt at averting the situation or mending the quarrel. Much as he apprehends its absurdity, he knows it must continue until Kreisler and Bitzenko are satisfied with the outcome. Asking himself what he would do if he were in Soltyk's shoes, Tarr ruminates:

> Kreisler was waiting at the door of the Café. If the Pole got up and went out, he would once more have his face smacked. His knowledge of Kreisler convinced him that that face would be smacked all over the Quarter, at all hours of the day, for many days to come. Kreisler, unless physically overwhelmed, would smack in public and in private until further notice. He would probably spit in it, after having smacked it, occasionally. So Kreisler must be henceforth fought by the Pole wherever met. Would this state of things justify the use of a revolver? No. Kreisler should be maimed. It all should be prepared with great thoroughness; exactly the weight of the stick, etc. The French laws would allow quite a bad wound. But Tarr felt that the sympathetic young Pole would soon have Bitzenko on his hands as well. Bitzenko was very alarming. (*T* 258)

The solutions which come to Tarr's mind are all violent and, even though it is still too early for him to appreciate the value of this insight, he has just seen how the plague of violence works. Aggression breeds aggression, and if the provoker is persistent enough, the chances of avoiding a conflict are practically non-existent. Seduced by the logic of reciprocity, one can easily get caught up in a cycle of escalating events, with new people joining in, and the hostilities becoming ever more intense.

Quite predictably, Soltyk and his companions are unable to leave Kreisler's and Bitzenko's provocation without response. In the "heroic, very solemnly official atmosphere of ladies' 'honour' and the 'honour' of gentlemen" (*T* 252), with all eyes turned on them in anticipation, and with the "scorching compress" (*T* 252) of the blow branded on Soltyk's cheek, they become convinced that facing the challenge is the only acceptable reaction. "This is the best thing to do" (*T* 259), thinks Staretsky, putting himself at Bitzenko's disposal at the beginning of the negotiations; a few moments later Soltyk arrives at the same conclusion, offering to "fight the German clown":

> Soltyk has made up his mind. . . . He did not regard this as a duel, but a brawl, ordered by the rules of "affairs of honour." If a drunken man or an apache attacked you the best thing to do would be to fight. If he offered to "fight you fair"—putting it in that way—then that would be the best thing too, no doubt. (*T* 261)

As the Polish party reach the unanimous decision to confront Kreisler, the process of their contamination is completed. Even Tarr, who apprehends the "tragic trend" that the situation has assumed, subscribes to their sentiment: with memories of his own hostile encounter with Kreisler still vivid, he has no difficulty understanding Soltyk's motivations. As he muses to himself, "How angry that man must be to do that" (*T* 262), his recognition of the power of aggression marks his surrender to the plague.

Not a duel but a brawl

The duel scene—the climax and the moment of greatest violence in the novel—occurs in the middle of the section ominously entitled "Holocausts." The scene is the point at which simmering antagonisms erupt, Soltyk's destiny as a sacrificial victim fulfils itself, and Kreisler's trajectory towards suicide irrevocably begins. It is in this particular scene that Lewis's portrayal of violence reaches its most poignant tones: the duel strikes the reader most of all, not with the gruesome outcome, but with its absurdity, unpredictability, and chaos. The notion that aggression is synonymous with the ultimate defeat of reason has been repeatedly suggested throughout the novel, but now it is plainly spelt out: whether a condemning moral judgement or a bewildered observation, the depiction of the duel clearly points to the futility and destructiveness of violence, its inadequacy in solving conflicts and dispersing tensions, and its entirely irrational foundations.

Lewis's choice of a duel as a vehicle for rendering his view on violence seems particularly relevant as duels are by definition meant to be a civilised, orderly form of aggression. Just how fallacious and self-contradictory such a concept must be is emphasised throughout the entire scene. Instead of a chivalric confrontation of two gentlemen, seeking satisfaction by arms over a matter of honour, we are presented with a lurid farce in which aggression runs roughshod over the duel's prescribed code of conduct, causing "wild bodies" to clash in a random brawl that ends in an accidental murder. The scene foregrounds numerous aspects of violence—its rationalization through rituals and heroic mythology, its attractiveness and tendency to spread, its absurdity, and the ease with which it can spin out of control. All this becomes a part of a more general reflection upon the breakdown of reason that accompanies violent acts as the physical mechanism of the body asserts itself, and human beings transform into automata governed by instinct.

It is fitting that the duel and the dramatic events that follow should take place without the presence of Tarr, the novel's only protagonist who represents, however inadequately, the values of the mind. His disappearance from the novel's action is tantamount to a withdrawal of rational supervision: it heralds the imminent release of beastly impulses and the movement of the narrative towards anarchic dissolution. The scene belongs wholly to Kreisler and to those who have failed to escape the plague of violence; their sinister potential can now realise itself without any intervention on the part of the non-infected characters. The action moves from metropolitan Paris to "a piece of waste land, on the edge of a wood, well hidden on all sides" (*T* 267). This more "natural" scenery helps to bring out the "natural" man, of whom Lewis, similarly to Conrad and in contrast to Lawrence, does not think very highly. A moment of crisis takes his protagonists back to the prehistoric condition of a barbaric past: as they yield to aggressive drives, they experience a nightmare regression, a paralysis of the intellect that pulls them towards the absurd.

Lewis's representation of the duel thus deliberately robs it of all the glory that such events may possess in the popular imagination. The text makes it clear from the beginning that Kreisler's confrontation with Soltyk is a contemptible affair that bears no relation to the honour code of the social elite; in fact, the idea of duelling as such is being put into question. Any attempts at investing it with heroic significance are immediately exposed as rationalisation of violent impulses and ruthlessly satirised, as in the following fragment when Kreisler invokes his noble ancestry to justify his "right" to use aggression against Soltyk:

> He remembered with eagerness that he was a German gentleman, with a *university education*, who had never worked, *a member of an honourable family!* He remembered each detail socially to his advantage, realising methodically things he had from childhood accepted, and never thought of examining. But he had gone a step further. He had arbitrarily revived the title of Freiherr that, it was rumoured in his family, his ancestors had borne. With Bitzenko he had referred to himself as the Freiherr Otto Kreisler. Had the occasion allowed, he would have been very courteous and gentle with Soltyk, merely to prove what a gentleman he was! But, alas, nothing but brutality (against the grain—the noble grain—as this went!) would achieve his end. (*T* 263)

In the absence of strong reasons for undertaking violent action, Kreisler constructs a personal chivalric ethos, incorporating the past with its structures of legitimacy and extending them into the present. His invented aristocratic pride is the only rationale he possesses,[90] and so he clings to it, playing the part of "a raving snob whose social dignity [Soltyk] had wounded" (*T* 264). Similarly, Bitzenko, the other aggressor, propagates a false image of himself by spreading stories of his prowess and exploits as a duellist. He is also greatly concerned with duelling etiquette, but only in the initial stage, as the arrangements for the duel are being made (later, when the whole affair ends in chaos, he grows less exacting and gets carried away by the violent spectacle). Both heroic mythology and an emphasis on ritual, hierarchy and titles are for Lewis only a cover-up for a penchant for aggression; they help to make violence appear honourable and justified, thus lending it a cultural sanction. In this respect, there is a parallel between the adversaries in *Tarr* and the "gentlemen in silk hats" of Winnie Verloc's fearful imaginings in *The Secret Agent*: the men's ostensibly civilised dress and conduct are just meant to hide the unbecoming truth of killing. Yet it must not be forgotten that Kreisler has never retrieved his frac from the pawnshop, and thus symbolically remains an outcast from the social class indulging in this sort of theatricality of revenge.

Additionally, Kreisler's and Bitzenko's weakness for grandiosity is contrasted with their simultaneous inclination to treat the duel as a kind of boyish adventure, "a satisfactory little affair" (*T* 257) and an opportunity to let off steam. Throughout the "Holocausts" sequence they are repeatedly compared to children, "little boys . . . in preparation for some mischief" (*T* 264), who seem to be blind to the sordid reality of the incident taking place at their instigation. With their minds captivated by an idée fixe, they do not reflect on the possible consequences of their actions, but stubbornly proceed to get their way:

> It was a whim, a caprice they were pursuing, as though, for instance, they had woken up
> in the early morning and decided to go fishing. They were carrying it out with a dogged
> persistency, with which our whims are often served. (*T* 266-267)

On arrival at the duelling site their childishness intensifies and gets ever more caricatural, as if emotional regression was directly proportionate to the proximity of danger. The scene is peppered with instances of their immature reactions, such as Bitzenko's indulgent testing of the pistols despite the fact that it might attract the police, Kreisler's demand of a sweet when he sees his adversary surreptitiously swallowing tranquillizers ("I want a ju-jube. Ask Herr Soltyk!," *T* 271), the bickering about whether the duel should

---

90   Kreisler's aristocratic pretences are also interesting in the context of Lewis's critique of Nietzsche. The philosopher is held responsible for the spread of the warrior ethos in bourgeois Germany, and for awakening "the will to power" in the most mediocre of men. In the 1915 Preface to *Tarr*, Lewis writes: "Nietzsche's books . . . have made "aristocrats" of people who would otherwise have been only mild snobs or meddlesome prigs . . . they have made "expropriators" of what would have otherwise been Arsène Lupins: and they have made an Over-man of every vulgarly energetic grocer in Europe" (*T* 13).

take place or not, the offer to withdraw the challenge for the price of a kiss, or, finally, the bewilderment with which Soltyk's death is greeted ("It was hardly a real corpse at all," *T* 276). Even as the realisation of the tragedy sets in, the aggressors are unable to take responsibility for their actions but, rather like a gang of young hooligans, they run away in different directions to escape the police. After a successful flight, Bitzenko reads the afternoon newspaper account of the whole affair with "infantile solemnity and calm" (*T* 277).

What is particularly fascinating about the duel scene is the ease with which Kreisler and Bitzenko dictate conditions to the Polish party and shape events according to their own liking. Soltyk and his companions, initially disinclined to fight and seemingly more rational than their challengers, take very little time to be provoked to violence. Kreisler's astonishing behaviour—childish, but also curiously bordering on the homoerotic[91]—strikes them as so offensive that they forget themselves. The duelling etiquette breaks down before the duel properly begins; Soltyk rushes out to throttle Kreisler, and then everybody joins in what appears to be a regular battle: "Meanwhile a breath of absurd violence had smitten everywhere. . . . The field was filled with cries, smacks, and harsh movements" (*T* 273).

In a moment of abandon, Lewis's protagonists begin to resemble automata, entirely subservient to the mechanism of their bodies. Their sensitivity to the world is not located in the activity of thought, but, as Michael Levenson rightly observes, "in the reflex of a nervous limb, the recoil of the hand, the spasms of the back and shoulders."[92] According to Lewis, human beings who follow their natural impulses become indifferent like robots and therefore unswerving in their destructiveness and cruelty. Alienated from human emotion, they not only have no difficulty in inflicting violence on others, but grow rigorous and unstoppable with it. The usually civilised Soltyk, who, treated to the "honey" of Kreisler's insults suddenly transforms into an "engine," "overcharged with fuel" (*T* 273), is an ideal example of such relentless, mechanistic efficiency:

---

91   As in many other scenes, here too Lewis foregrounds the connection between violence and sexuality. Kreisler's demand of a kiss from Soltyk and his sudden realisation that "He *loved* that man! But because he loved him he wished to plunge a sword into him, to plunge it in and out and up and down" (*T* 270) have been usually associated with the Oedipal nightmare that Kreisler has experienced. Paul O'Keeffe explains that on the duelling ground Soltyk becomes conflated in Kreisler's mind with his stepmother fiancée, transforming into "an unmanageably complex object of hate and (explicitly sexual) love." See: "Afterword" in Wyndham Lewis, *Tarr: the 1918 Version*, ed. Paul O'Keeffe, (Santa Rosa: Black Sparrow Press, 1996). It is also possible to see Kreisler's "love" of Soltyk in Freudian, or even Girardian terms: Soltyk is Kreisler's "ideal ego," a role model and unattainable ideal. For this reason he must evoke conflicting emotions of both hatred and love, very much like the Prussian officer in a short story by D.H. Lawrence.

92   Levenson, *Modernism and the Fate of Individuality*, 126.

His hands were electrified. Will was at last dashed all over him, an arctic douche. The hands flew at Kreislers throat. His nails made six holes in the flesh and cut into the tendons beneath. Kreisler was hurled about. He was pumped backwards and forwards. (*T* 272-273)

Just in case the humans managed to break out of their automated trance and regain their analytical capacities—which indeed they do at one point, "dusting their trousers, arranging their collars, picking up their hats" (*T* 273) and resolving to abandon the duel—real machines are there to ensure the triumph of destructive forces. Anticipating contemporary science fiction fantasies, Lewis incorporates technological gadgetry into his vision of violence: it is partly thanks to the menacing presence of modern inventions that blood is finally spilt on the duelling ground. On the fateful morning, Kreisler is woken up by the sound of an alarm clock exploding into his ear; then destiny is signalled again by an ominous car which "so plainly knew what it wanted" (*T* 268); eventually, at the critical moment when Kreisler tries to force the duel on the retreating Poles, his Browning pistol discharges by mistake. Machines facilitate the enactment of bloodthirsty imaginings, and—unlike humans—never fail in their absurd murderous mission.

In the end, it is the human beings, not the machines, who appear to have lost control of the whole situation. Its tragic finale takes them aback and engenders a universal feeling of disappointment: Kreisler regrets that everything happened too fast and he had no time to revel in the violence, Bitzenko regrets there was not enough carnage to glare upon, the Poles regret the stupid and unnecessary loss of their friend. Reality proves so different from what they had expected that they are incapable of any response apart from sobbing or running away, and their child-like reactions confirm for the reader their ultimate defeat.

A conclusive representation of the absurdity of violence, the duel scene, however, gains special significance if one considers the time in which *Tarr* was written. The climactic clash of the novel may be seen as an allegory of the Great War, which, in popular mythology, also began as a crusade saturated with glory and honour, or as an armed version of a sporting event that seemed to work according to a clearly defined set of rules and to a principle of fairness.[93] Advertised as strenuous but attractive, the war made the European masses rush eagerly to battlefields but soon brought

---

[93]   For historical accounts of the Great War mythology, see for example: Paul Fussell, *The Great War and Modern Memory*, (Oxford: Oxford University Press, 1975), 25-29 and chapter 4, "Myth, Ritual and Romance," Modris Eksteins, *Rites of Spring: The Great War and the Birth of the Modern Age* (London: Black Swan, 1989), 120-126, or Samuel Hynes, *A War Imagined*, (London: Pimlico, 1992), the Introduction, ix-xiii, part I, "The Lights Go Out: 1914-15" and part II, "The Turning Point: 1916."

about profound disillusionment as the reality of combat came crashing down. Its unprecedented brutality, intensified by the use of technologically advanced weapons, took combatants by surprise and evoked a sense of betrayed idealism and lost innocence. All this is in a way prefigured in the duel scene when violence gets out of hand and everything turns out differently than planned. The rules of duelling are not observed, the adversaries display aberrant behaviour, machines become instruments of fate and gain control over the people who use them. What began as, at least in part, an idealistic enterprise ends as a bloodbath: violence is easy to initiate and—once initiated—impossible to control, a reflection to which millions of lives lost in the Great War lend an overwhelmingly terrifying weight.

Only a game, too

Soltyk's accidental death marks Kreisler's transition to the last stage of his Parisian adventure, and, consequently, his adventure with life. With blood on his hands, he is ready for the definitive step he has so many times threatened to take—the ultimate act of violence that settles at last his accounts with the world. Throughout the narrative he has been characterised by a condition of deadness (he inhabits a room resembling a funeral vault, we learn that "his life might have been regarded as a long and careful preparation for voluntary death" (*T* 164), before the duel he thinks of himself as "a man who [is] practically dead to all intents and purposes, one mass of worms" (*T* 264)), so suicide is for him a natural course of action and a logical conclusion to his erratic existence. Nevertheless, as Kreisler prepares to take his own life, he is still reluctant to reflect upon the consequences of his actions and dies, just like Verloc in *The Secret Agent*, with a sense of mild disbelief that this should be happening to him:

> He began slowly drawing off his boots. He took out the laces, and tied them together for greater strength. Then he tore several strips off his shirt and made a short cord of them. He went through these actions deliberately and deftly, as though it were a routine and daily happening. He measured the drop from the bar of the ventilator, calculating the necessary length of cord, like a boy preparing the accessories of some game. It was only a game, too. He realised what these proceedings meant, but shunned the idea that it was serious. Just as an immoral man with a disinclination to write a necessary letter, takes up the pen, resolving to begin it merely, and writes more and more until it is in fact completed, so Kreisler proceeded with his task. (*T* 285)

By killing Kreisler, Lewis ultimately confirms the pointlessness of violence, underscoring the fact that apart from destroying the people towards which it is directed, it also destroys the individual indulging in it. Although, as Michael Levenson observes, "one does not go to Wyndham Lewis to renew a commitment to humane values,"[94] the implication of the novel's denouement seems quite clear: the path of violence is a path of madness and death, and those who choose it deserve to meet a tragic end.

94 Levenson, *Moderrism and the Fate of Individuality*, 144.

CHAPTER IV

Humanity in a *Cul-de-sac*: *Women in Love* as an Epic of Sacrificial Crisis

The last century [the 19th] was the winter of the West, the victory of materialism and scepticism, of socialism, parliamentarianism, and money. But in this century blood and instinct will regain their rights against the power of money and intellect. The era of individualism, liberalism and democracy, of humanitarianism and freedom, is nearing its end. The masses will accept with resignation the victory of the Caesars, the strong men, and will obey them.

Oswald Spengler, *Decline of the West*

In the year when Wyndham Lewis went to the Front, D.H. Lawrence completed *Women in Love*. Although originally conceived as a sequel to *The Rainbow,* the novel proved quite different in mood from anything Lawrence had produced before: revising it, he doubted the possibility of ever finding a publisher for such a gloomy, "end-of-the-world"[95] narrative. While his previous work seemed to him "destructive-consummating," the new creation was "purely destructive"[96] and, in its vision of a declining civilisation, poignantly resonant of the war *Zeitgeist*. Always interested in man's inherent darkness but perhaps more than other modernists inclined to value it as a creative force, Lawrence found himself grievously affected by the developments of contemporary history. The war shook his faith in human capacity for spiritual rebirth through crisis, and, as he made clear in one of his letters, the transition from *The Rainbow* to *Women in Love* reflects this change of perspective:

---

95   Lawrence to Carswell, 7 November, 1916, *The Collected Letters of D.H. Lawrence,* Harry T. Moore, ed., (London: Heinemann, 1962), Vol.I, 482.

96   Lawrence to Frank, 27 July, 1917, *The Collected Letters of D.H. Lawrence,* Vol.I, 519.

About *The Rainbow*: it was all written before the war, though revised during Sept. and Oct. 1914. I don't think the war had much to do with it—I don't think the war altered it, from its pre-war statement . . . I knew I was writing a destructive work, otherwise I couldn't have called it *The Rainbow*—in reference to the Flood. . . . And I knew, as I revised the book, that it was a kind of working up to the dark sensual or Dionysic or Aphrodistic ecstasy, which does actually burst the world, burst the world-consciousness in every individual. What I did through individuals, the world has done through the war. But alas, in the world of Europe I see no Rainbow. I believe the deluge of iron rain will destroy the world here, utterly, no Ararat will rise above the subsiding iron waters. There is great *consummation* in death, or sensual ecstasy, as in the Rainbow. But there is also death which is the rushing of the Gadarene swine down the slope of extinction. And this is the war in Europe. We have chosen our extinction in death, rather than our Consummation. . . . There is another novel, sequel to *The Rainbow*, called *Women in Love* . . . This actually does contain the results in one's soul of the war...[97]

Informed by wartime pessimism, *Women in Love* foregrounds aggression and animosity as hallmarks of modern society. The notion of the ubiquitous struggle between individuals, explored by Lawrence in earlier works, is revisited from the standpoint of the cataclysmic upheaval raging in Europe. Lawrence's erstwhile Nietzschean and futurist fascinations, so clearly visible in *The Rainbow*,[98] are corrected by his consciousness of the historical moment: the celebration of the Dionysic gives way to a reflection upon the futility of conflict and violence. The war is not fought in the novel's pages, but its destructive potential is written into the plot, projected onto the imagery and internalised in the characters. The result is a lurid picture of humanity enacting a death wish through senseless strife which can only cause scars and damage—just as it happened when

---

97   Lawrence to Frank, 27 July, 1917, *Collected Letters of D.H. Lawrence*, Vol.I, 519.

98   Lawrence's engagement with Nietzsche, and later with futurism, seems to have shaped his pre-war perception of conflict as an essentially positive phenomenon. *The Rainbow*, with its language of "Dionysic and Aphrodistic ecstasy," celebrates the perpetual battle of wills taking place within the Brangwen family. The tensions between Will and Anna, Ursula and Skrebensky are destructive but also satisfying—a far cry from the "pure destructiveness" of *Women in Love*. As Andrew Harrison argues in *D.H. Lawrence and Italian Futurism*, the representation of conflict in *Women in Love* is marked by self-consciousness which seems to be a product of the war *Zeitgeist*: "In *Women in Love* the war's presence in the text elicits a quite different tone and atmosphere: one of 'bitterness' (*WL* 485). The Futurist process of coming through violence to new forms of life is now subordinated to a sense of tragic fate and wasteful destructiveness. . . . The violence associated with Futurism no longer forms a prelude to to a new vision; rather, this violence is felt in stillborn, frozen, wounded characters." Andrew Harrison, *D.H. Lawrence and Italian Futurism: A Study of Influence,* (Amsterdam: Rodopi B.V., 2003), 132.

European countries became involved in mortal combat. Adrift in alienating landscapes, first industrial and then frozen and desolate ones, Lawrence's protagonists indulge in unproductive interpersonal battles, emblematic of the entropy which rules their world. Energy is expended, often violently, but as Gudrun observes in the opening chapter, "nothing materialises, everything withers in the bud" (*WL* 2). In contrast to *The Rainbow, Women in Love* substitutes all hope for progress or renewal with a countdown to a potential exhaustion: violence that is amiss will not have a cathartic effect, or bring about a radical turn in the course of events—rather, it will leave behind a sense of irreparable waste and irresolvable chaos.

In the late stages of composition, Lawrence considered calling his novel *Dies Irae* (Day of Wrath), but abandoned the idea, probably because the religious connotations of this title, even if apocalyptic, carry the promise of a brighter future. In the world of *Women in Love* wrath is indeed a prevalent phenomenon, though it rarely leads to anything positive. The characters are angry, and conflict is for them almost as natural as breathing: they willingly set themselves in opposition to others and seem to enjoy the physical and mental violence that transpires. Unlike *The Secret Agent* or *Tarr,* Lawrence's book features no obvious villains who would stir up trouble in an otherwise peaceful community; rather, aggression is distributed more or less evenly among all the protagonists. It appears to be a defining characteristic of a dysfunctional generation, as represented by the strong-willed Brangwen sisters, tyrannical Gerald, misanthropic Birkin, domineering Hermione, promiscuous Pussum and diabolical Loerke. Violence is even ciphered in some of the characters' names, evoking belligerent heroes of Norse and Teutonic myths. For example, Ursula is named after a Nordic equivalent of the Roman goddess Diana, Gudrun—after a witch who murdered her husband, and Loerke—after Loki, a god of mischief and evil. The name "Gerald" also has an interesting etymology, as it originates from the Germanic roots *gēr*, spear, and *waltan*, to rule. Like the ancient narratives such names bring to mind, Lawrence's novel revolves around the questions of struggle, submission and domination, treating them as part and parcel of existence. Wrath and the will to power are the chief motivating forces for the characters, so it is certain that victims will fall, and a bloodletting is not a matter of *if*—but *when*.

It has to be said, however, that it is not so much the inevitability of violence, but the normality and ubiquity of it that turns *Women in Love* into a truly unsettling text. Addressing issues inherent in the state of modernity in 1916, Lawrence goes a step further in his representation of human aggression than Conrad and Lewis before him. It is possible to view the works of the three writers in terms of progression: what at first was a marginal phenomenon, limited to the underworld and hidden from sight, begins to resurface with ever greater frequency and urgency, until it becomes an inescapable attribute of everyday life. From one novel to the next the characters grow more and more defiant, and there is simultaneously an increasing acceptance of aggressive behaviour in their environment, as though the intensifying militarism of early twentieth-century Europe found an immediate reflection in the cultural production of its time. If outbreaks of violence in *The Secret Agent* were rare and quite spectacular, in *Tarr* perhaps less so, but still out of the ordinary, in *Women in Love* they are almost commonplace. In Lawrence's fictional world no one makes much ado when Pussum jabs a knife across her companion's hand, Hermione strikes Birkin with a paperweight, and Gerald wants to strangle Gudrun in a fit of jealousy. This is a culture of confrontation, a civilisation bent upon war, where the capacity to act aggressively is honed in daily interactions, such as lovers' bickering, tensions between miners and industrial owners, or high society conversations resembling "a rattle of small artillery" (*WL* 73). The characters revel in demonstrations of their strength and draw pleasure from subduing other people, animals and nature. Even friendship is expressed through a wrestling match—a clean, hard-fought athletic contest which, although not really aggressive in itself, celebrates masculine prowess and is a way of asserting one's potential to dominate others. In terms of the novel's formal construction, acts of violence are no longer "big events" upon which the plot is hinged. Compared to *the Secret Agent* or *Tarr*, their character seems more episodic: they do not upset chronology or grow progressively more intense, but remain in the background, as sure to happen as the sun rising in the east.

The veneer of civilised pretence that the protagonists of *The Secret Agent* and *Tarr* found so suffocating, does not present such a problem in *Women in Love* because there is not much commitment to keeping it up. Appearances can no longer conceal the principle of basic mistrust by which the inhabitants of the novel's world operate, assuming, as Rupert Birkin does, that "[w]hat people want is hate—hate and nothing but hate. And in the name of righteousness and love, they get it." (*WL* 112). The common expectation is that others may only offer a negative version of social experience, hence the most appropriate question to be addressed to a close friend is the one Birkin asks of Gerald: "Do you ever consciously detest me—hate me with mystic hate?" (*WL* 46). This can hardly be called a climate conducive to the restraint of violent impulses, for when individuals explode in anger, they just confirm what other people have suspected them of anyway. The prevalent *Weltanschaung* in the novel, in which an informed reader will recognise an amalgam of Freudian, Nietzschean and social Darwinist beliefs, offers a justification for aggressiveness, deeming it necessary for self-preservation in a hostile environment. A lack of hope in humanity causes patience to evaporate more quickly, so inner bonds frequently snap and the pessimistic view of man's nature is borne out, becoming a kind of self-fulfilling prophecy. In fact, what entraps Lawrence's characters is not the falsity of social norms, but rather a sense of their own inescapable baseness, and an apprehension of the same negativity in others.

The assumption that human beings are depraved at their core and naturally violent reflects "the bitterness of the war" which, according to the authorial introduction to *Women in Love*, is to be "taken for granted"[99] in the protagonists. Cultural pessimism of exactly this kind was widespread at the time the novel was written, and had also been popularised by a vast range of ideological visions long before the global conflict of 1914 became reality. Discourses of innate violence were present in the work of such philosophers as Hobbes, Schopenhauer, Spencer or Nietzsche and, in the course of the history of Western thought, they were used for various purposes, for example to explain the need for coercive social norms and civilisational restraint. At the same time, as many theorists of violence have observed, the idea of aggression as a natural given offered a powerful rationalisation of the impulse to dominate and destroy. Responsibility for violent behaviour could be shifted onto factors outside human volition and consciousness. The implications of this position became evident at the beginning of the twentieth century when people like the German militarist General von Bernhardi began invoking the concept of "biological necessity" in defence of unabashed aggression, and to make the case for the forthcoming war:

> War is a biological necessity of the first importance, a regulative element in the life of mankind which cannot be dispensed with, since without it an unhealthy development will follow, which excludes every advancement of the race, and therefore all real civilization. . . . War gives a biologically just decision, since its decision rests on the very nature of things. . . . Struggle is, therefore, a universal law of Nature, and the instinct of self-preservation which leads to struggle is acknowledged to be a natural condition of existence. "Man is a fighter." Self-sacrifice is a renunciation of life, whether in the existence of the individual or in the life of states, which are agglomerations of individuals. The first and paramount law is the assertion of one's own independent existence.[100]

Lawrence's novel focuses on a society which has internalised such beliefs. Although its confidence in civilisation has dwindled, it still embraces competitive mentality in all aspects of life. For the protagonists of *Women in Love*, aggression and the will to power cannot be questioned, they are simply there in the world, and any attempts to deny this must be dismissed as sentimental idealism. Gerald Crich's reflection on his position as an

---

99   "The bitterness of the war may be taken for granted in the characters." D.H. Lawrence, unpublished "Foreword" (1919) to *Women in Love*, reprinted in several paperback editions. See for example: D.H. Lawrence, *Women in Love*, (London: Penguin 1995), 485.

100   Friedrich von Bernhardi, *Germany and the Next War*, (1911), Allen H. Powles, ed., (Honolulu: University Press of the Pacific, 2001).

industrial magnate well exemplifies this attitude, and bears an uncanny resemblance to the social Darwinist sentiments quoted above:

> He did not care about the equality. The whole Christian attitude of love and self-sacrifice was old hat. He knew that position and authority were the right thing in the world, and it was useless to cant about it. They were the right thing, for the simple reason that they were *functionally necessary*. (*WL* 207, italics mine)

The "functional necessity" of crushing others in the process of self-realisation is a guiding principle in most relationships in the novel. When Hermione launches her attack on Birkin, it is because she lacks *lebensraum* and perceives his presence as an obstacle on her way to happiness: "[H]e was the wall. She must break down the wall— she must break him down before her, the awful obstruction of him who obstructed her life to the last." (*WL* 92) Similarly, Gudrun and Gerald find themselves trapped in an "eternal see-saw, one destroyed that the other might exist, one ratified because the other was nulled" (*WL* 410). It is as if people have lost the capacity for striking a balance and seeking mutual satisfaction through compromise: the only mode in which they can function is that of excess, of extreme egoism that does not take account of anyone and anything.

Although usually a champion of the natural (even if violent) man, in *Women in Love* Lawrence is rather critical of the predatory relations existing in the modern world. The novel is pervaded with a deep sense of unease about civilisational change fundamentally transforming human attitudes, causing people to become more beastly than they need to be. While in Lawrence's earlier texts conflict and abusive behaviour seem at least partly excusable, the violence represented in *Women in Love* is of a slightly different calibre. The difference is subtle and sometimes difficult to pin down, but taking Lawrence's hint about "purely destructive" and "destructive-consummating" novels, we can perhaps see the point. The critic Michael Black, who has studied Lawrence's philosophical output, observes a distinction present in his work between violent actions committed "in hot blood," "as an expression of one's profound being" and those related to "social consciousness and social will,"[101] the former type being of course more acceptable than the latter. This is a valid argument, though not always applicable to what we find in *Women in Love*, with the exception of Birkin's insight about the murderer and the murderee. Of course, the novel is war-engendered, and certainly construes intensified aggression as a feature of a decomposing society, but there is also a new anxiety in Lawrence concerning the potential for unreflective cruelty to be found in man. What comes under the spotlight is the omnipresence of

---

101   Michael Black, ed., *D.H. Lawrence: The Early Philosophical Works*, (Cambridge: Cambridge University Press, 1992), 134.

misanthropy and malice, as well as emotional atrophy and lack of compassion, manifesting itself in "the cold devil of irony" (*WL* 439), freezing human souls. Additionally, just as in Wyndham Lewis's *Tarr*, violence is seen as a realisation of some purely mechanical force, something that cannot bring true satisfaction, for it is not about confrontations—measuring one's strength against another's—any more, but about the removal of obstacles and the exercise of control. In Girardian terms, all the sacredness of violence is lost, there is no glory or heroic daring in it, only degradation for all parties involved. Stabbing, throttling and delivering blows are represented as spasmodic bodily jerks, giving momentary pleasure, but not drawing the protagonists any closer to the Lawrentian ideal of "fullness of being." *Women in Love*, much more than other Lawrence's texts, is about a world thrashing in meaninglessness, and such is also the violence engendered in it. It does not make much sense biologically, ideologically, or even psychologically; it occurs because people can no longer cope, but there is nothing teleological about it.

One thing that seems connected with this purposelessness of violence is the persistent thought running through the novel that humanity has exhausted itself. Afflicted by "a fearful nausea" (*WL* 79), "the nausea of dissolution" (*WL* 174), "the nausea of stirring the old broth" (*WL* 387), Lawrence's characters are not capable of giving direction to their lives. Whatever they do, they are bound to regret it; to use a phrase from Conrad, they are always faced with "a choice of nightmares."[102] Violence and aggression are possible options, as futile as anything else, and only confirming the hopelessness of one's predicament. In search of an explanation for modernity's violent disposition, we may resort to the thoughts of Gerald Crich, anticipating his own failure and hence burning with pathetic rage. They can be taken as a motto of the generation depicted in the novel, as well as Lawrence's more universal diagnosis of the condition of modern man:

> He did not inherit an established order and a living idea. The whole unifying idea of mankind seemed to be dying with his father, the centralising force that had held the whole together seemed to collapse with his father, the parts were ready to go asunder in terrible disintegration. Gerald was as if left on board of a ship that was going asunder beneath his feet, he was in charge of a vessel whose timbers were all coming apart.
>
> He knew that all his life he had been wrenching at the frame of life to break it apart. And now, with something of the terror of a destructive child, he saw himself on the point of inheriting his own destruction. And during the last months, under the influence of death, and of Birkin's talk, and of Gudrun's penetrating being, he had lost entirely that mechanical certainty that had been his triumph. Sometimes spasms of hatred came over him, against Birkin and Gudrun and that whole set. (*WL* 201)

---

102   Conrad, *Heart of Darkness*, 62.

An omen of universal dissolution

Among the many aggressive figures in *Women in Love*, Gerald Crich deserves separate treatment because of the symbolic function conferred on him as the novel's tragic hero. Much critical weight has been placed on the fact that he is not just a psychological portrait of an individual, but rather "a representative consciousness, a product of the most advanced civilisation the world had yet seen, but one which has exploded into an apparent apocalypse of violence and destruction in the bloodiest war of human history."[103] It is his destiny which epitomises the fate of the modern male, and the false promise of the brave new industrialised world where economic production and machine-like efficiency have supplanted the outmoded ideals of Christianity and democracy. Introduced into the plot as an able, rational man of the twentieth century, "a Napoleon of industry" (*WL* 52), with good prospects for a career in politics, Gerald is shown to dwindle away to spiritual emptiness and eventually collapse, meeting his death among the snowy sterility of the Alps. A question worth exploring is whether and in what way his failure is prompted by his aggressiveness, and also how Lawrence's allegory contributes to the general view of violence emerging from the text.

Throughout the novel, Gerald is consistently associated with the races of the north, their impressive efficiency and invincible will. He is a blond, Aryan type, clearly a descendant of the brave peoples whom the late nineteenth- and early twentieth-century anthropology deemed the earth's conquerors and pioneers of civilisation.[104] With his "clear northern flesh" and "pure arctic" glisten, he seems a fine specimen of an *Übermensch,* someone who "[does] not belong to the same creation as the people about him" (*WL* 8). The perfection of his physique is accompanied by a masterful attitude, determination and boldness of vision—features which seem to predestine him to greatness and which enhance the expectation of flawless performance in every sphere of his life. And yet, with equal consistency, Lawrence's text undermines the confidence in Gerald's potential success: we learn at the outset that he is tainted with the curse of Cain and has brotherly blood on his hands, that he has never had a friend[105] and that there is

---

103   Ken Newton, University of Dundee. "Women in Love" in: Robert Clark, ed., The Literary Encyclopedia, 1 Nov. 2002, The Literary Dictionary Company, 24 June 2005. <http://www. litencyc.com/php/sworks.php?rec=true&UID=8853>

104   Ideas of the northern origins of civilisation and the racial superiority of the Aryan race were quite popular in turn-of-the-century Europe. It is likely that Lawrence was familiar with some publications propagating Aryanism and Nordicism, such as for example G.H. Rendall's *The Cradle of the Aryans* (London, 1889), which pointed to Scandinavia as the original seed-bed of the Aryans.

105   This is what Mrs Crich is greatly concerned about. She mentions this fact in a conversation with Birkin: "I should like [Gerald] to have a friend. He has never had a friend" (*WL* 18). Birkin suspects that Gerald's accidental killing of his brother may be the reason why people avoid him—he is contaminated with violence and therefore evokes anxiety.

some "sinister stillness in his bearing," suggestive of "the lurking danger of his unsubdued temper" (*WL* 8). Later we see him enter into reductive relationships with women, exploit his workmen and cause harm to animals. He begins to appear in the context of death (of his sister, then of his father) and himself grows deathly, as if his northern coldness were causing him to gravitate towards the iciness of cemeteries and tombs. All this lends a disquieting edge to the image of Gerald as a modern superhero and prophesises the fall of the race which has thought itself the most fit to govern the earth.

Gerald's northerness acquires a specifically symbolic significance in the light of Rupert Birkin's apocalyptic vision of humanity's future. Imagining two polarised modes of self-destruction, one for the northern, the other for the southern hemisphere, Birkin predicts that "[t]he white races, having the arctic north behind them, the vast abstraction of ice and snow, would fulfil a mystery of ice-destructive knowledge, snow-abstract annihilation" (*WL* 232). While the people of the south are destined for dissolution through purely mindless, sensual experience, the north must perish as a result of its excessive trust in reason and the worship of mechanical order. Finding in Gerald a quintessence of abstract sterility, Birkin reads his presence as a prophetic sign:

> Birkin thought of Gerald. He was one of these strange white wonderful demons from the north, fulfilled in the destructive frost mystery. And was he fated to pass away in this knowledge, this one process of frost-knowledge, death by perfect cold? Was he a messenger, an omen of the universal dissolution into whiteness and snow? (*WL* 232)

Described by an oxymoronic phrase, Gerald the "wonderful demon" signals the direction in which triumphant modernity is heading. He is a strange kind of omen, for many of his qualities can actually be perceived as admirable. Even Birkin, perspicacious enough to intimate Gerald's destructiveness and what it may lead to, remains under the spell of his charismatic being. This, by extension, is also a feature of the culture that Gerald embodies, because it too, glittering and attractive on the surface, has kept people oblivious to the rot eating at its core. Consequently, the northern races have enthusiastically paved the way for their extinction and now, on the brink of an abyss, they face no choice but to rush down the slope—much like the Gadarene swine that Lawrence's wartime letter mentions with reference to the combatant nations.

Explaining, through Gerald, where civilisation has taken a false step, Lawrence points to several of its characteristics which, welcomed as indicators of progress, have put it on a path towards dissolution. The northern man's cardinal sin is that he has denied his life-force by yielding to the pressures of mechanised industrialism. Nature—important only insofar as it can be exploited—has been harnessed in the service of culture and reduced to "raw stuff" upon which people work their design. The balance between body and mind has shifted towards the latter, and a new, rationalist ethic has emerged, based on the belief that human intellect can will everything into submission. Violence plays an important role in this paradigm, for to sustain the fiction of the all-powerful and self-sufficient ego, one must continually exert control, even by applying physical force. The whole northern vision of civilisational advancement is built around ideas of expansion and domination, wilful imposition of order, crushing instincts and fighting resistant matter, all for maximum profit and a sense of unconditional victory.

Both a product and an embodiment of this culture, Gerald seeks satisfaction through assertion of power. In every action he undertakes, in the personal sphere as well as in industry, there is an element of more than human aspiration, a desire for absolute mastery that leaves no room for compromise. When in one of the early chapters of the novel he is swimming in a pond, he feels "immune and perfect" and "exult[s] to himself, because of his own advantage, his possession of a world to himself" (*WL* 38). He would like to achieve the same degree of control over the earth when as a ruthless entrepreneur he tears coal out of its interior, over live creatures, such as his mare and Winifred's rabbit, which he restraints with his powerful grip, and even over women, whom he is ready to "destroy . . . rather than be denied" (*WL* 370), as in the scene of his lovemaking to Gudrun. The fantasy of supremacy becomes Gerald's driving force and sole motivation, so he emerges from the novel as a Nietzschean type, faithful to no value beyond the dictate of his will. His *Weltanschaung*, together with its practical implications, is best spelt out in the descriptions of his management of the family mines:

> The will of man was the determining factor. Man was the archgod of earth. His mind was obedient to serve his will. Man's will was the absolute, the only absolute. And it was his will to subjugate Matter to his own ends. The subjugation itself was the point, the fight was the be-all, the fruits of victory were mere results. It was not for the sake of money that Gerald took over the mines. He did not care about money, fundamentally. He was neither ostentatious nor luxurious, neither did he care about social position, not finally. What he wanted was the pure fulfilment of his own will in the struggle with the natural conditions. His will was now, to take the coal out of the earth, profitably. The profit was merely the condition of victory, but the victory itself lay in the feat achieved. (*WL* 203-4)

To ensure his victory over recalcitrant matter, Gerald resorts to the machine, which essentially functions as an extension of man's will. He wants to be a high priest of a new mechanical order, an orchestrator of a modern transformation that will put things right once and for all, making the world function effectively. The family business he reorganises serves him as a testing ground, and the community of miners is like a modern society in miniature. Rejecting his father's paternalistic management methods, Gerald supplants them with a form of technocracy, where workers are subordinate to "the Godhead of the great productive machine" (*WL* 205) and themselves treated as "mere mechanical instruments" (*WL* 210). Modernisation leaves no room for Christian sentiments or charitable deeds; instead, it promises to transcend human imperfection and creates an illusion of greater control. Having fallen for it, Gerald begins to view himself and others in purely instrumental terms:

> He did not care what they thought of him. His vision had suddenly crystallised. Suddenly he had conceived the pure instrumentality of mankind. There had been so much humanitarianism, so much talk of sufferings and feelings. It was ridiculous. The sufferings and feelings of individuals did not matter in the least. They were mere conditions, like the weather. What mattered was the pure instrumentality of the individual. As a man as of a knife: does it cut well? Nothing else mattered.
>
> Everything in the world has its function, and is good or not good in so far as it fulfils this function more or less perfectly. Was a miner a good miner? Then he was complete. Was a manager a good manager? That was enough. Gerald himself, who was responsible for all this industry, was he a good director? If he were, he had fulfilled his life. The rest was by-play. (*WL* 203)

Curiously, Gerald's mechanistic fantasy does not prove too difficult in realisation: even though it is unnatural and sterile, his colliers seem to accept it. It is almost as if they too found this abuse of will appealing and wished to be sacrificed in the service of abstractions:

> The men were satisfied to belong to the great and wonderful machine, even whilst it destroyed them. It was what they wanted. It was the highest that man had produced, the most wonderful and superhuman. They were exalted by belonging to this great and superhuman system which was beyond feeling or reason, something really godlike. Their hearts died within them, but their souls were satisfied. It was what they wanted. Otherwise Gerald could never have done what he did. He was just ahead of them in giving them what they wanted, this participation in a great and perfect system that subjected life to pure mathematical principles. This was a sort of freedom, the sort they really wanted. It was the first great step in undoing, the first great phase of chaos, the substitution of the mechanical principle for the organic, the destruction of the organic purpose, the organic unity, and the subordination of every organic unit to the great mechanical purpose. (*WL* 210)

By becoming a part of the new order, "strict, terrible, inhuman, but satisfying in its very destructiveness" (*WL* 210), Gerald's miners follow their supervisor into the drift of northern cultural entropy. Their fate not only reflects the disastrous effects of industrialism but is uncannily parallel to the experience of World War I soldiers, or may even be taken as a prediction of the fascism which was to sweep Europe in the next decade. Under the guise of progress and liberation, chaos and death are ushered in, but people are too intoxicated with abstract concepts to be able to prevent a catastrophe. Driven by their own, or somebody else's *Wille zur Macht*, they fail to realise that the superhuman status they strive for is not an improvement, but a denial of humanity, and that a technological framework does not make the world better or more manageable.

A combination of the crude assertion of power, the fall out of oneness with nature and the repression of humanism must, in Lawrence's eyes, bring about a cultural breakdown. Connected with it is an intensification of aggression, or even the emergence of a new type of cruelty, suited to the demands of ice-corrupted times. As the novel's central exemplar of dissolution, Gerald is representative also in this respect: he is endowed with a disturbing capacity to inflict abuse without getting hot under the collar. His violence is not of a passionate kind that Birkin would associate with the southern, or African, temperament; rather, it is cool and calculated, more in accordance with—to use Joyce's phrase—the modern vivisective spirit.[106] It is defined as "perfect, good-humoured callousness," "strange malice, glistening through the plausible ethics of productivity" (*WL* 46), and it seems to be stemming from the northern tendency to restructure the entire world as an object of control. Gerald's abstract take on reality, his emphasis on mechanised efficiency and the assumption of his own superiority facilitate his distancing from fellow human beings, whom he feels entitled to use as he pleases. Unable to respond from the heart, he acts according to his quantitative mindset, treating production and creation as values in their own right. If all that matters is "the great social productive machine" where he happens to be "a controlling, central part" (*WL* 207), then crushing others on the way to goal realisation appears justifiable. The implications of such an attitude are quite ominous, for the grand myth of progress and the appeal of mechanical order can both cover up and serve as incentives for the murkiest of crimes and most cruel acts of exploitation.

By making the connection between modernity and cruelty, Lawrence advances the same argument as his contemporary namesake, Phillip K. Lawrence, who in his book *Modernity and War: The Creed of Absolute Violence* blames modern industrialism, scientism and instrumental reason for making possible the horrors of mechanised warfare and organised genocide. Among the leitmotifs of modernity, he enumerates "dominion

---

106   Cf. James Joyce, *Stephen Hero*, Theodore Spencer, ed., (Norfolk, CN: New Directions, 1963), 90. "The modern spirit is vivisective. Vivisection itself is the most modern process one can conceive. The ancient spirit accepted phenomena with a bad grace. The ancient method investigated law with the lantern of justice, morality with the lantern of revelation, art with the lantern of tradition. But all these lanterns have magical properties: they transform and disfigure. The modern method examines its territory by the light of the day."

over other peoples and lands, the place of science in the construction and ordering of the polity, and the rise of technocratic and instrumentalist rationalism."[107] He also claims, developing an earlier thesis of Adorno and Horkheimer, that Western culture, affected by the Enlightenment dialectic, in which domination over nature ends in domination over human beings,[108] began using the idea of "progress" as an excuse for violence and for subjugation of "lesser" men. Technological innovation enabled humans to be more efficiently vicious, and thus modernity, rather than fulfilling its promise, degenerated into a new barbarity.

Gerald, whose life's trajectory reflects the deathly vector of modern Europe, already betrays symptoms of this barbarous viciousness in childhood. First, he kills his brother while playing with a gun—a symbolic instrument with which the northern man established his supremacy over various places on Earth. Then, during the miners's strike, he watches the soldiers pacify the protesters and longs to join them in the shooting. Emerging into adulthood, he wants to "try war" and then "travel into the savage regions"— that is, to gather the experience of a soldier and coloniser, necessary to become a full-blown representative of his aggressive culture. As one early critic of *Women in Love* pointed out, there is a thread of cruelty running through Gerald's life, a sequence of more or less significant events and circumstances which foster his violent inclinations and determine his tragic fall:

> Gerald Crich, the industrialist and woman idolator, is traced back to the boy who killed his little brother by a fateful accident; and to the baby who had a brutal and vindictive nurse. The thread is fine that D.H. Lawrence brings from invisibility, a slender thread of forgotten things that are fate, fateful because forgotten and because they are integral to a man's life and the quality of his being. The thread of cruelty flashes in view as Gerald Crich grinds down his Arabian mare, tearing her with spurs, forcing the quivering animal to stand at a crossing as a freight train passes. It is the link with the woman, fated by his nature and her own to destroy him.[109]

Gerald's northern upbringing, in conjunction with his personal history and natural aggressiveness, turns him into a domineering, possessive figure who reduces all relationships to a struggle of wills. His yearning for control, utopian and impossible in its essence, makes him doomed from the outset and causes him to destroy himself and others only to meet "death by

---

107   Phillip K. Lawrence, *Modernity and War: The Creed of Absolute Violence*, (London: Palgrave Macmillan, 1997), 87.

108   Phillip Lawrence's book draws on the critique of Enlightenment proposed by Horkheimer and Adorno in one of the most celebrated texts of the Frankfurt school, *Dialectic of Enlightment* (1976).

109   Herbert J. Seligmann, *D.H. Lawrence: An American Interpretation,* (New York: T. Seltzer, 1924), 14-15.

perfect cold." The thread of cruelty ultimately leads him to a teleological impasse, symbolised by the frosty landscape of the Tyrolese Alps: "He saw the blind valley, the great *cul de sac* of snow and mountain peaks, under the heaven. And there was no way out." (*WL* 370)

At the time Lawrence was writing his text, Gerald's destiny was fulfilling itself for thousands of young men on the battlefields of Flanders. Western civilization, despite vaunted claims of progress, seemed to have arrived at a dead end, and the collective bloodletting failed to provide a panacea for accumulated frustrations. The miseries of Ypres, Verdun and the Somme offered no lasting solutions, just as the scarring of the mare's sides or the strangling grip around Gudrun's neck proved no cure for Gerald's existential nausea. Girard's thesis rings true both with regard to historical reality and the reality dramatised in the novel: when the sacred dimension of violence is lost, there can only be destruction without consummation—just sterile, pointless brutality. Its spasmodic eruptions punctuate the entropic flow, but cannot avert or alleviate it.

Tellingly, Lawrence makes Gerald disappear into the oblivion of the snow with a thought which was, at that moment in history, well-recognizable to most Europeans: "I didn't want it, really" (*WL* 436). These are Kaiser Wilhelm's words, uttered on the outbreak of World War I. Later, they are repeated by Birkin over Gerald's frozen body, this time the historical allusion is made explicit, despite the general absence of references to the War in the novel:

> "I didn't want it to be like this—I didn't want it to be like this," he cried to himself. Ursula could but think of the Kaiser's: "Ich habe es nicht gewollt." She looked almost with horror on Birkin (*WL* 442).

In this way, the story of the European disaster is woven into Lawrence's apocalyptic vision. Collapsing in the snow with Gerald is the splendidly arrogant culture which, in pursuit of greater good for the world, has moved into conflict and death. The Kaiser's statement in the mouths of Lawrence's protagonists becomes a belated regret, no doubt genuine, that things have not quite turned out as planned.

Mutual hellish recognition

Gerald Crich functions as a representative modern male and a harbinger of doom, but he is not the novel's villain in the sense that Kreisler is in *Tarr*. In Lawrence's vision, evil influence is not concentrated in a single figure, and aggressiveness is a widespread phenomenon, only varying in intensity from one person to another. Significantly, it breaches the divide between the sexes: with the rise of the New Woman, the northern man gains a partner (and an adversary), who, like himself, has a taste for violence and is capable of using others for egoistic purposes. In the world of *Women in Love*, when it comes to the perpetration of violent acts, Gerald takes the lead, but women are just behind, asserting their will with knives, stones and open hands. They display a matching degree of cynicism and icy coldness, and their outbursts, far from being hysterical and incoherent, consistently ram home the message that female subjugation is at an end. Preoccupied with the ambition "to have, to own, to control, to be dominant" (*WL* 182), modern women reflect and partake in the general arrogance of their culture, thus failing to counterbalance its suicidal trend.

The critic Helen Wussow detects a tone of accusation in Lawrence's writing, concerning the role of female aggressivity in the demise of contemporary society. She observes that Lawrence "forges a connection between industrialism and the insincere, flirtatious, modern woman,"[110] who indulges in man-manipulation and boldly reaches for the perceived privileges and benefits of maleness. This poses a threat to the state of equilibrium, which, for Lawrence, can only be gained through a marriage of opposites. Wilful and calculative females tip the scales of the north further towards the cerebral, the abstract and the sterile, "leaving the experience all in one sort" (*WL* 231) and aggravating the general impasse. The modern man and the New Woman are bound by a relationship of mimetic rivalry: there is mutual recognition and knowledge between them, but no genuine concern for each other. The conflicts which transpire are a waste of resources and a denial of life, but because innocence has been lost on both sides and the hold of mimetic desire is too strong, no one wishes to step back and forsake their aspirations.

The women of *Women in Love*—Gudrun, Hermione, Pussum, Mrs Crich, Diana, even the generally peaceful Ursula and the very young Winifred—are all touched by the malaise of modernity. The first three are openly aggressive and cocksure, the others are slyly manipulative, possessive and unsentimental. They perceive the males in their environment as rivals (Gudrun), obstacles (Hermione), half-men (Pussum) or bullies (Ursula). They are prepared to suffer loss coldly, without emotional devastation, like Gudrun who accepts Gerald's death with irony, or Winifred, who is barely moved by the disappearance of a favourite pet. When drowning, they pull their men along, like Diana Crich, and when insecure, they launch an unexpected attack, like Pussum at the restaurant table. Disconnected from nature and corrupted by culture, Lawrence's women have little warmth to give: they are sparing in affections (Hermione, Gudrun), aloof towards their inferiors (Winifred, Gudrun) and opposed to the idea of charity (Mrs Crich). Finally, having supplanted Eros with Thanatos, they exhibit a negative attitude towards motherhood: the Brangwen sisters "get no feeling whatever from the thought

---

110   Helen Wussow, *The Nightmare of History: The Fictions of Virginia Woolf and D.H. Lawrence*, (Betlehem: Lehigh University Press, London: Associated University Press, 1998), 23.

of bearing children"[111] (*WL* 3), Pussum experiences pregnancy as something "beastly" (*WL* 58), and Mrs Crich, once a fervent mother, realises that her children "scarcely mean anything to her" (*WL* 199).

In this generally unflattering picture of modern women, one character stands in the foreground as especially threatening: Gudrun Brangwen, a stylish bohemian and the symbolic counterpart to Gerald in that she too functions as an omen of cultural decadence. Like Gerald, Gudrun possesses uncanny charisma and treacherous potential; what is more, the destructive wilfulness of modern art which she represents parallels the modern denaturing industrialism. Throughout the novel, Lawrence consistently underscores the similarity of Gudrun's and Gerald's natures: "they were of the same kind, he and she, a sort of diabolic freemasonry subsisted between them" (*WL* 108). Their relationship is a clear case of Girardian mirroring that must inevitably conclude in a violent clash: the object of their rivalry is power and since neither of them can bear subjugation, they get locked in a struggle of wills, resembling an "eternal see-saw" (*WL* 410).

From the novel's earliest moments, Gudrun's enchantment with Gerald seems to be mingled with envy: the features which first attract her attention have to do with his self-contained ease and social advantage. For example, the sight of him swimming naked in the pond induces in Gudrun a vehement regret that as a woman she would not be able to follow suit without risking her reputation. Ursula, witnessing the same scene, observes that the water must be cold and unpleasant, but her sister is not discouraged— she perceives the male world as thoroughly attractive:

> Gudrun envied him almost painfully. Even this momentary possession of pure isolation
> and fluidity seemed to her so terribly desirable that she felt herself as if damned, out
> there on the high-road.
> "God, what it is to be a man!" she cried.
> "What?" exclaimed Ursula in surprise.
> "The freedom, the liberty, the mobility!" cried Gudrun, strangely flushed and brilliant.
> "You're a man, you want to do a thing, you do it. You haven't the *thousand* obstacles a
> woman has in front of her." (*WL* 38)

What Gudrun would like to do is to blur the gender difference—if not to be a man, then at least to be *like* one—a desire that Lawrence obviously finds very alarming. Without ascribing a mysogynist intent to him, one may interpret his attitude as concern over the possible side effects of such emancipation: the question he raises is whether in the process of achieving male-like status, women will not assume the worst of male qualities

---

111   Ursula, as we know from *The Rainbow*, induced the miscarriage of her child by Skrebensky by jumping off a tree.

and perpetuate the worst of male follies. The type of northern manhood represented by Gerald is, after all, deathly and deplorable, so for the woman to imitate it means to plunge civilisation into an abyss.

The violence which will ensue from the Gudrun-Gerald tension is signalled very early, through a series of voyeuristics exchanges arousing Gudrun's lust for power. One of them, the railway scene, involves the sight of blood and the subjugation of a live creature as Gerald forces his beautiful Arab mare to withstand the clatter of a passing train. Gudrun is absolutely mesmerised by this abusive spectacle; she watches Gerald with "black-dilated, spellbound eyes" (*WL* 99) and feels as if she were about to swoon:

> Gudrun looked and saw the trickles of blood on the sides of the mare, and she turned white. And then on the very wound the bright spurs came down, pressing relentlessly. The world reeled and passed into nothingness for Gudrun, she could not know any more. . . . Gudrun was as if numbed in her mind by the sense of indomitable soft weight of the man, bearing down into the living body of the horse: the strong, indomitable thighs of the blond man clenching the palpitating body of the mare into pure control; a sort of soft white magnetic domination from the loins and thighs and calves, enclosing and encompassing the mare heavily into unutterable subordination, soft blood-subordination, terrible. (*WL* 99-100)

Many critics interpret the incident in terms of sexual symbolism; it has been speculated that Gudrun undergoes an orgasmic experience when watching the mare being coerced into submission between Gerald's thighs. While the affinity between violent abandon and sexual excitement is frequently suggested in Lawrence's writings (cf. the scene when Hermione attacks Birkin, when Gerald throttles Gudrun, or when the orderly in *The Prussian Officer* story rushes upon his captain), Gudrun's reaction here is more likely to indicate fascination with Gerald's power. Rather than identify with the object of Gerald's coercion, Gudrun would prefer to play the part of the master of the show. In contrast to Ursula, she is not disgusted by what she sees, but attracted to the pleasures resulting from the imposition of one's will. This remains in agreement with Girard's insight about the mimetic nature of human aggressiveness: we learn to act brutally by way of imitation. Spectacles of violence are so compelling that even viewers who are morally revolted by the deed (Ursula) do not avert their eyes, whereas for people with a greater proclivity to violence (Gudrun), watching is a form of mental rehearsal, a method of gaining self-confidence through experiencing vicariously what one wishes to experience directly.

Gerald's gratuitous display of cruelty becomes for Gudrun a moment of initiation and the point at which the rules of their interaction are delineated. She embraces them wholeheartedly and soon signals her yearning for domination in the symbolic cattle scene. The act of scaring a herd of bullocks prepares the way for further aggression and helps Gudrun to overcome fear and dismay as she slaps Gerald on the face. An "unconquerable desire for deep violence" (*WL* 153) which she feels then will revisit her time and again in her dealings with Gerald, and he will respond with the same kind of destructive frenzy. In store for them, there is a strange game of attraction and repulsion, based on mimetic responses and discomforting awareness of their similarity:

> Gudrun looked at Gerald with strange, darkened eyes, strained with underworld knowledge, almost supplicating, like those of a creature which is at his mercy, yet which is his ultimate victor. He did not know what to say to her. He felt the mutual hellish recognition. And he felt he ought to say something, to cover it. . . . There was a league between them, abhorrent to them both. They were implicated with each other in abhorrent mysteries. (*WL* 221)

As in a classic Girardian double bind, in the relationship between Gudrun and Gerald imitation becomes rivalry, and flattery becomes aggression. Each partner knows what to expect from the other, but the ultimate "abhorrent mystery" they must share—and come to terms with—is that only one of them can emerge victorious from the struggle.

Lawrence resolves the conflict in Gudrun's favour: she ultimately proves to Gerald that "he could never cow her, nor dominate her, nor have any right over her" (*WL* 405). As their involvement with each other is spiralling to a climax, Gudrun reaches such levels of defiance that it proves too much even for Gerald. Her sneering disdain and icy cynicism become Gerald's death by perfect cold—however unemotional and inadequate he is himself, he eventually falls victim to a sick, unfeeling relationship and is killed by his own weapon. In a truly Girardian finale, Gerald feels reduced to a sacrificial offering, "exposed, like an open flower," "torn apart and given to Gudrun" (*WL* 390). The New Woman has violated his most intimate secrets: she has learnt from him and used the knowledge to destroy him. Taking past *femme fatales* for her models, she wants to emulate Cleopatra, who "reaped the essential from a man," "harvested the ultimate sensation, and threw away the husk" (*WL* 392). Once all that Gudrun needs has been obtained from Gerald, he can be discarded for the sake of a new attraction, the sculptor Loerke, who appears to pose a greater challenge.

The fact that Gerald dies in the snow and Gudrun survives has a symbolic dimension as well; it can be taken as Lawrence's bitter comment on the empowerment of women which followed from World War I and which occurred, terribly enough, at the cost of slaughtered men. As Joanna Bourke and other historians have argued,[112] the war was crucial in disrupting former expectations of both femininity and masculinity, it also heightened tensions between the sexes. To some degree, *Women in Love* reflects the anxieties of a society in transition.

---

112   See: Joanna Bourke, *Dismembering the Male: Men's Bodies, Britain and the Great War,* (London: Reaktion Books, 1996), 23-24, 192-198.

Apart from men and women behaving aggressively in relationships, what interests Lawrence is the more general destructive and self-destructive impulse present in human beings. It is the same kind of sentiment that Conrad investigates through the figure of the Professor, and Lewis, to a certain extent, through Kreisler and Tarr. Manifesting itself in a number of ways—fascination with morbidity, genocidal fantasies, dread of the masses, misanthropy, suicide—it seems to bear out Freud's theory of the thanatic drive which causes humans to act against the interest of their own species. *Women in Love* constantly inflects this idea as it portrays mankind exhausted with itself and yearning for liberation from life's oppressiveness; in keeping with the apocalyptic thrust of the novel there is persistent talk of dissolution, nausea, flux, corruption and "universal defilement" (*WL* 108). The characters desire death for others, and subconsciously also for themselves; their imagination reworks visions of annihilation and finds symptoms of decline in their physical environment—the scarred countryside, the sordid industrial towns, the barren cul-de-sac of mountain peaks. *Dies Irae* is reenacted on virtually every page, and there is no promise of a rainbow to cheer the reader up.

The sense of an ending registered by the protagonists of Lawrence's fictional world becomes translated into all kinds of antisocial and antihuman attitudes and practices. Misanthropy is widespread, and the presence of fellow human beings is perceived as a threat. For this reason Gerald seems "always to be at bay against everybody" (*WL* 42), and Hermione strives "to make herself invulnerable, unassailable, beyond the reach of the world's judgement" (*WL* 11). At the same time, there is a tendency to ignore others, best visible in Mrs Crich who chooses not to care about the people gathered at her home for the wedding reception. This approach is met with complete understanding by Birkin, the novel's prime misanthrope and prophet of doom, openly declaring that "[p]eople don't really matter" and that "it would be much better if they were just wiped out" (*WL* 18).

Birkin's apocalyptic discourse sets the tone for the novel, so that the end result is pretty sinister—even Lawrence, having finished his book, declared that he hardly dared to read it again. Seen by many critics as a mouthpiece for Lawrence's ideas, Birkin is burdened with the task of verbalising the universal death wish and providing commentary on a dying civilisation.[113] He pronounces man "a mistake" and humanity "a dead letter" (*WL* 48). In his most bitter moments, he resembles the Professor of *The Secret Agent*, relishing in hypothetical genocide, and full of abhorrence at the swarming multitudes:

---

113 Indeed, the tenor of many of Birkin's utterances remains in agreement with that of Lawrence's wartime letters. Like Conrad with his abominable Professor, Lawrence uses Birkin to express his disappointment with mankind, trying at the same time to expose the dangers of misanthropic nihilism.

Well, if mankind is destroyed, if our race is destroyed like Sodom, and there is this beautiful evening with the luminous land and trees, I am satisfied. ... Let mankind pass away—time it did. (*WL* 48)

Birkin watched the country, and was filled with a sort of hopelessness. He always felt this, on approaching London. His dislike of mankind, of the mass of mankind, amounted almost to an illness. (*WL* 49)

"If we want hate, let us have it—death, murder, torture, violent destruction—let us have it . . . I abhor humanity, I wish it were swept away. It could go, and there would be no *absolute* loss, if every human being perished tomorrow. The reality would be untouched. Nay, it would be better." . . . I would die like a shot, to know that the earth would really be cleaned of all the people. It is the most beautiful and freeing thought. (*WL* 108)

Unlike in Conrad, Birkin's attitude is not represented as unique or extremely pathological; in *Women in Love* mass death is on everybody's mind. Gerald, for example, imagines a potential mass grave in the depths of Willey Water, pointing out, with what one critic sees as "the volumetric knack of a skilled engineer,"[114] that "[t]here's room under that water there for thousands" (*WL* 156). Similarly, Gudrun would be quite keen to wipe the world clean: one suspects she could make a perfect terrorist, since her destructive fantasies usually dawn upon her during public gatherings. In church during the Criches' wedding she would like to see the crowd of colliers' wives "annihilated, cleared away, so that the world was left clear for her" (*WL* 8), and at the water party she feels she "could have killed" (*WL* 136) the girls tittering behind her back. She has the same murderous feelings towards the contemptible coterie at "this whirlpool of disintegration and dissolution" (*WL* 332)—the Pompadour Café. Later, in her discussions with Loerke, she visualises a man-induced end of the world, executed by means of a perfect explosive:

As for the future, that they never mentioned except one laughed out some mocking dream of the destruction of the world by a ridiculous catastrophe of man's invention: a man invented such a perfect explosive that it blew the earth in two, and the two halves set off in different directions through space, to the dismay of the inhabitants: or else the people of the world divided into two halves, and each half decided *it* was perfect and right, the other half was wrong and must be destroyed; so another end of the world. (*WL* 396)

---

114   David Bradshaw, ed., Introduction to *Women in Love*, (Oxford: Oxford University Press, 1998), xv.

All these exercises of imagination, although not literally threatening, are illustrative of the potential for intraspecific aggression, buried at the level of the individual psyche. They give a clear signal that a cosmic catastrophe is already ticking in human hearts, and when it finally explodes, it will be more than welcome.

The modern man's longing for self-destruction becomes evident also in the murderer-murderee theory that Birkin expounds to Gerald early in the novel. Believing that everything in the world "h[angs] together, in the deepest sense" (*WL* 20) and that there are no accidental occurrences, Birkin invests individual death with a universal significance. In his opinion, people are the puppets of fate, actors and victims realising a preset scenario. If violence dogs Gerald wherever he goes, it must be his destiny, and his unacknowledged innermost desire:

> "No man," said Birkin, "cuts another man's throat unless he wants to cut it, and unless the other man wants it cutting. This is a complete truth. It takes two people to make a murder: a murderer and a murderee. And a murderee is a man who is murderable. And a man who is murderable is a man who in a profound if hidden lust desires to be murdered."
>
> "Sometimes you talk pure nonsense," said Gerald to Birkin. "As a matter of fact, none of us wants our throat cut, and most other people would like to cut it for us—some time or other—"
>
> "It's a nasty view of things, Gerald," said Birkin, "and no wonder you are afraid of yourself and your own unhappiness."
>
> "How am I afraid of myself?" said Gerald; "and I don't think I am unhappy."
>
> "You seem to have a lurking desire to have your gizzard slit, and imagine every man has his knife up his sleeve for you," Birkin said. (*WL* 26)

By coaxing Gerald to look his fate in the eye, Birkin is in fact playing a deadly game himself. He encourages Gerald in his suicidal end, indirectly murdering the person he needs and admires, so as to find himself feeling incomplete and desolate at the novel's end. After all, it is psychologically quite puzzling that Birkin, sensing his friend's ominous potential, in fact does very little to prevent his failure. When the climactic moment approaches, he flees from the Tyrol with Ursula, leaving Gerald at the mercy of Gudrun and Loerke, his final executioners who will ensure that the tragic destiny is fulfilled. The gesture is only explicable in the light of the universal dissolution which forces individuals to discard what is vital to them and thus unwittingly slit their own gizzard.

At one point or another, virtually everyone in *Women in Love* acts against their own interests, in this way pursuing their self-destructive quest. Gerald is the first to go, for he is a man with the mark of Cain, a murderer who—just like Lewis's Kreisler—must now become a murderee. But as he disappears among the mountain peaks, it is certain that others will follow. His friends, some left behind with a shadow of survivor guilt, some blindly proceeding into the vortex of corruption, do not seem to have a rosy future before them. Hermione, estranged from Birkin, has returned to her vacuous existence, incomplete, and with no one to close the "secret chink in her armour" (*WL* 10). Gudrun will probably find her destruction in Loerke, who is confident that he will "penetrate into [Gudrun's] inner darkness, find the spirit of the woman in its inner recess and wrestle with it there, the central serpent that is coiled at the coil of life" (*WL* 416). There also seems to be every likelihood that Ursula and Birkin's marriage will be negatively affected by the fact of Gerald's death, with Birkin's hopes for an "eternal union with a man" (*WL* 444) forever frustrated. Each destined to rot in his or her own private hell, Lawrence's characters must join in the flux, because they have made the wrong choices, and because they have been born into a decadent era.

Perhaps to offset the pessimistic tenor of his text, at the novel's end Lawrence allows Birkin a final word of consolation. However feeble it seems from the perspective of the lost generation depicted in the book, at least it tries to make sense of, as well as see beyond, the modern self-destructiveness:

> The eternal creative mystery could dispose of man, and replace him with a finer created being. Just as the horse has taken the place of the mastodon. . . . If humanity ran into a *cul de sac* and expended itself, the timeless creative mystery would bring forth some other being, finer, more wonderful, some new, more lovely race, to carry on the embodiment of creation. The game was never up. The mystery of creation was fathomless, infallible, inexhaustible, forever. Races came and went, species passed away, but ever new species arose, more lovely, or equally lovely, always surpassing wonder. The fountain-head was incorruptible and unsearchable. It had no limits. It could bring forth miracles, create utter new races and new species, in its own hour, new forms of consciousness, new forms of body, new units of being. To be man was as nothing compared to the possibilities of the creative mystery. To have one's pulse beating direct from the mystery, this was perfection, unutterable satisfaction. Human or inhuman mattered nothing. The perfect pulse throbbed with indescribable being, miraculous unborn species. (*WL* 441-442)

It is up to the reader to decide if the myth of eternal return really answers the questions about human violence posed by Lawrence's novel. The reservations voiced by the critic David Bradshaw with respect to the above fragment are probably well worth considering: "[H]ow much authority does [Birkin] have left at the end of *Women in Love*? The truth is that Gerald's spectacular and portentous death lives with the reader in a way which Birkin's numbing bombast does not. . . . [A]lthough Birkin was meant to have the leading role in *Women in Love* (as the protagonist who is most "acutely alive"), it is the degenerate Gerald and Gudrun who steal the show."[115] Apparently, just as was the case with *Tarr*,

---

115   Bradshaw, ed., Introduction to *Women in Love*, xxii.

what gives weight to the novel is the most nihilistic aspect of the whole message. The bleaker the vision, the truer it rings, and the closer it gets to our idea of the modern.

Lawrence used to believe that "one sheds one's sickness in books"[116]; in *Women in Love* he seems to have shed the sickness of the entire Western civilisation. A product of a mind attuned to the growing brutality of the world, it is perhaps the most socially and historically perceptive of all Lawrence's fictional creations. It pictures a society in the state of sacrificial crisis, full of aggression and potentially volatile. It also captures the spirit of the war, fought at the time of the novel's writing and not having any cathartic effect. Finally, it forewarns, albeit to a large degree unwittingly, of the ideological dangers looming on the horizon. Depicted in his work is a humanity which, exhausted with its own corruption, becomes susceptible to populist fantasies of the final solution. Birkin's talk of the end of a cycle, as well as his hopes for the new races, miraculous finer beings to take over the Earth, is a desperate attempt to render disaster triumphant, an attempt which, if carried to its logical conclusion, acquires a rather disquieting overtone.

---

116   From Lawrence's letter to A.W. McLeod of October 1913, *The Collected Letters of D.H. Lawrence*, Harry T. Moore, ed., (London: Heinemann, 1962), Vol.I, 234.

CONCLUSION

If there existed a ranking of the most unpleasant fictions that British—or even European—modernism ever produced, the three novels discussed in this study would most likely occupy some of the top positions. Unsparing in laying bare the darkest of human impulses, *The Secret Agent*, *Tarr* and *Women in Love* can make the reader flinch with understandable discomfort: one almost wishes, like Lawrence when reading Forster, that "a bomb would fall and end everything."[117] This, after all, is a most natural reaction to a world plunged into a sacrificial crisis, and a wish well known to the violent protagonists who must confront the murky realities dreamt up for them by the merciless authors. Yet, as Girard suggests, one should strive to overcome the mimetic impulse and look man's inhumanity in its ugly face, forsake the temptation of nihilism and try to comprehend the mechanisms behind the worst of all social plagues, which is violence. What Conrad, Lewis and Lawrence offer is an attempt at unveiling, an exposure of what we would prefer to close our eyes to—and, curiously, the Greek word for "unveiling" is "apocalypse."

Not easy to read, the three novels were not easy to write in the first place. As with other creative works, *The Secret Agent* cost Conrad a depression. "I feel quite wretched and overdone not with work but with the anxiety this beast Verloc causes me,"[118] he complained in a letter to J.B. Pinker in October 1906, and years after the novel's completion, when adapting it for the stage, he would still experience qualms about the "sordid surroundings and moral squalor of the tale" (*SA* xxvii). Wyndham Lewis, after the eight-year period of struggling with *Tarr*, was "incidentally glad" to "vomit Kreisler

---

117   *The Collected Letters of D.H. Lawrence*, Vol.II, 799.

118   *The Collected Letters of Joseph Conrad: Volume III, 1903-1907*, Frederick R. Karl *et al.*, eds., (Cambridge: Cambridge University Press, 1988), 367.

forth," like "one big germ more" (*T* 13, Preface), a germ which had been infesting his artistic conscience for too long. Similarly for Lawrence, whom we like to think of as a very fast and prolific writer, the work on *Women in Love* meant a prolonged creative tussle, marred by his experience of wartime, which he compared to "a sort of coma, like one of those nightmares when you can't move."[119] Upon finishing, he felt ambivalent, calling the novel both "wonderful and terrifying, even to me who have written it."[120]

So many things about writing these books must have been intense: the creative effort, the time of composition, the subject matter. And there is intensity in the reading, too, as Conrad's, Lewis's and Lawrence's tragic visions descend upon us, offering a glimpse of the chaos and violence that are often the flip side of human endeavour. If Terry Eagleton, quoted at the beginning of Chapter I of this study, is right to say that tragedy in the twentieth century mutates into modernism, then the three novels discussed here are very good examples of such a mutation. The role of tragedy, as Girard sees it, is to undermine the prevailing cultural messages, to go beyond the clear-cut polarised model of good and evil, to peep into the abyss which myths try to conceal. Through their engagement with violence, *The Secret Agent, Tarr,* and *Women in Love* accomplish exactly this, though they may lack the pomp and scale which marked their ancient counterparts.

The unveiling that Conrad, Lewis and Lawrence execute concerns the sacrificial crisis of their time, at first brewing slowly under the thin façade of civilisation and then gradually engulfing various aspects of modern life. Violence is identified as both the symptom and the product of the malady, likely to destabilise all norms and arrangements, and to disrupt the familiar order of things so that it could never be put to rights again. The three novelists seem to join their efforts in an attempt to warn their audiences about the possible outcome of the negative developments they observe. From one novel to the next, the unsettling diagnosis is delivered with greater urgency, accompanied by a growing realisation that not much can be done to avert the catastrophic trend. The sense of pessimism is proportionate to the degree to which violence dominates both the reality depicted in a given novel and the actual historical reality in which this novel was being written.

Arranged in chronological order, *The Secret Agent, Tarr* and *Women in Love* form an interesting triptych, representing stages in the evolving crisis. In Conrad's text, there are few visible marks of social disintegration, and violence remains a hidden threat, caged in potentially explosive individuals. If eruptions occur, they are sudden, surprising and serious in their consequences. There is also a strong belief in the cathartic and transformative power of violent actions: all those who plan and perpetrate acts of transgression treat them as means to improve their predicament, or change the world for the better. In

---

119   *The Letters of D.H. Lawrence: Volume II, June 1913-October 1916*, George J. Zytaruk *et al*, eds., (Cambridge: Cambridge University Press, 2002), 211.

120   *The Collected Letters of D.H. Lawrence*, Vol.I, 519.

Tarr, tensions in society are more noticeable, and what receives particular emphasis is the blatant aggressiveness of modern males. The novel's dominant metaphor is that of contagion: violence is captured in the process of spreading, as negativity radiating from a central disruptive figure catches on, and multiplies itself by way of reciprocal escalation. Outbreaks of aggression are less spectacular than those in *The Secret Agent*, but there is also greater tolerance of antisocial behaviour in the community. While in Conrad's imagined world civilisational restraints of violence are still in operation (the police manage to locate dangerous individuals and undertake at least some punitive or protective countermeasures), in *Tarr* such external control is weaker: despite the fact that duelling is an illegal practice, the clash between Kreisler and Soltyk takes place; the police never track Kreisler down after he has committed manslaughter; Bertha as a victim of rape remains silent about what happened to her. Violence is perceived more in physical than moral or ethical terms, it is simply a form of energetic discharge, a way to relieve pent-up emotions and stress. This trend is upheld in *Women in Love,* where aggression pervades daily interactions, becoming the norm rather than an aberration. Characters experience seizures of rage, turning livid in an instant and delivering a blow in the next moment, without any need for reflection or justification of their deeds. Represented largely as a reactive effect, violence emerges out of a sense of oppression generated by a modern mechanised society where relations are based on domination and exploitation. Because of its frequency and commonplace character, abusive behaviour is not transformative and does not alleviate discord—to use Girardian terms, it has become frustratingly profane.

Apart from reflecting the stages in the countdown to eventual disaster, the three novels make statements on human aggression, which constitute contributions to the early twentieth-century Western violence mythos. Each of the statements is unique, though there are many points upon which Conrad, Lewis and Lawrence converge, reflecting the attitudes particular to their historical moment. All three writers see modernity as an epoch of heightened aggressiveness and expect this negative potential to materialise in some catastrophic form. They envisage the existence of disillusioned or destructively inclined individuals who may wish to assert their presence by threatening others with extermination. Recognising the appeal that violent solutions possess, both in the eyes of social outcasts and ordinary members of society, the three modernists not only register the problems likely to beset the modern world, but also take responsibility to seek explanations of their origins.

The Secret Agent, the first of the novels to be written, combines the elements of both nineteenth- and twentieth-century thinking on violence. While seeing aggression as endemic to the human species, Conrad places considerable trust in the idea of civilization as a means (imperfect, but the only one we have) of restraining anti-social impulses. He emphasises the inescapability of coercive systems, but at the same time acknowledges the impossibility of exercising total control. Human existence is for him a continual struggle against the forces of anarchy and unreason: despite all efforts to satisfy our need for security and reassurance, there is always a risk of some "secret agency," threatening to betray us. Violence in *The Secret Agent* is represented as such—an "enemy within"—a haunting presence beneath a thin crust of morality, etiquette and refinement. Following the insights of late nineteenth-century anthropology, Conrad links violence to a retreat to savagery, and a failure of rational thinking, thus constantly reminding us that the illusions which sustain us rest on weak foundations. The mental structures that we build and the moral paradigms we take for granted can be undone in an instant; one thing that seems certain is the existence of primeval chaos into which everything can vanish, only to be blindly born anew. Violence, as a manifestation of the chaotic, will continue to frustrate human aspirations: the wish to transcend it is noble but ultimately futile. Just as we cannot interfere with the infernal machine to which Conrad likens our universe in one of his letters,[121] we cannot hope to switch off the bomb ticking within us, within our constructs, cognitive models and relationships.

In comparison to Conrad's, Lewis's attitude to violence is a little less fatalistic. *Tarr* construes human aggression as a plague which can be avoided if only we understand the mechanisms that bring it about. The novel's focus is on the mimetic character of our desires and on the ways in which negative emotions are allowed to spread. Unlike Conrad, Lewis does not see reason as an illusion but rather as our last resort, the only power that can save us from becoming ridiculous "wild bodies," slavishly following the dictates of instinct. Of all the three writers, Lewis seems to be the most sanguine advocate of ironic distance: his representations of violence are entirely vivisective, devoid of warmth or sympathy that would allow our identification either with the perpetrators or the victims of aggression. Lewis's message is ruthless but clear: those who yield to the madness of violence fully deserve the self-annihilation they bring upon themselves and should die their absurd deaths, like the contemptible puppet Otto Kreisler, choking with his own tongue as he commits suicide.

---

121 See Conrad's letter to Cunnighame Graham of December 1897: "There is a—let us say—a machine. It evolved itself (I am severly scientific) out of a chaos of scraps and iron and behold!—it knits. I am horrified at the horrible work and stand appalled. I feel it ought to embroider—but it goes on knitting. You come and say: "this is all right; it's only a question of the right kind of oil. Let us use this—for instance—celestial oil and the machine shall embroider a most beautiful design in purple and gold." Will it? Alas no. You cannot by any special lubrication make embroidery with a knitting machine. And the most withering thought is that the infamous thing has made itself; made itself without thought, without conscience, without foresight, without eyes, without heart. It is a tragic accident and it has happened. You can't interfere with it. The last drop of bitterness is in the suspicion that you can't even smash it. . . . It knits us in and it knits us out. It has knitted time, space, pain, death, corruption, despair and all the illusions and nothing matters." *The Collected Letters of Joseph Conrad: Volume I*, 425.

D.H. Lawrence's perspective on human aggression differs from that of Conrad and Lewis in that he trusts neither reason, nor civilisation, but at the same time refuses to demonise our proclivity to violence. He is the most likely to undermine the Hobbessian view of human nature and comes closest to acceptance of man's instinctual endowments. His novels draw attention to the fact that not all violence is deadly, and that anger is a natural reaction, part and parcel of being human. Nevertheless, as *Women in Love* seems to warn us, unhealthy relationships in society, excessive egoism and technological will to power can lead to pointless destructiveness, a waste of human resources and, ultimately, teleological impasse. To avoid self-exhaustion through unnecessary aggression, humanity should try to strike a balance between the icy sterility of reason and the consuming flames of passion, though as Lawrence's novel pessimistically suggests, we are quite incapable of attaining such an ideal equilibrium.

By taking part in the cultural discourse on human aggression, Conrad, Lewis and Lawrence not only register certain aspects of the violence mythos prevalent at their time, but also make attempts at changing some of the conventional attitudes and beliefs. A side effect of their engagement with violence is the fact that they help to domesticate this issue, by including it in the realm of high literature and by depicting acts of brutality and cruelty. Such was, however, the general direction in which modernist art and literature progressed; partly as a result of this, domestication and aestheticisation of violence became one of the features of twentieth-century culture. Perhaps the present status of violence in the Western cultural production—both of the high and the low brow kind (if such a distinction still exists)—is in part a consequence of the specific treatment of this subject by modernist artists and writers. We are inheritors of their legacy: after more than a century, modernism's intellectual capital has not been exhausted.

One common feature of *The Secret Agent, Tarr* and *Women in Love* that requires a special emphasis in this context, is the fact that even though the three novels domesticate the issue of violence, they nevertheless pass a moral judegement on it. All aggressive figures, perpetrators and orchestrators of violence in the three texts are eventually brought low, rejected, and relegated to the margins of society. Conrad, Lewis and Lawrence avoid siding with their villains or presenting violence as an object of enjoyment and celebration. The main transgressors of the three narratives—the Professor, Winnie, Kreisler, Gerald Crich—commit, or are meant to commit, suicide. In this way, the three novels communicate, in their own distinctive ways, an ethical message, showing violence as a solution that leads nowhere and must ultimately prove self-destructive.

Primary Sources

Conrad, Joseph. *The Secret Agent: A Simple Tale* (1907). The Cambridge Edition of the Works of Joseph Conrad. Eds. Bruce Harkness, S.W. Reid. Cambridge: Cambridge University Press, 1990.

-----. "Autocracy and War"(1905). In: *Notes on Life and Letters*. The Cambridge Edition of the Works of Joseph Conrad. Eds. J.H. Stape, S.W. Reid. Cambridge: Cambridge University Press, 2003. 71-93.

-----. *Heart of Darkness* (1899). Ware: Wordsworth Classics, 1995.

-----. *Joseph Conrad's Letters to R.B. Cunninghame Graham*. Ed. Cedric Watts. Cambridge: Cambridge University Press, 1969.

-----. *The Collected Letters of Joseph Conrad: Volume I, 1861-1897*. Eds. Frederick R. Karl *et al*. Cambridge: Cambridge University Press, 1983.

-----. *The Collected Letters of Joseph Conrad: Volume III, 1903-1907*. Eds. Frederick R. Karl *et al*. Cambridge: Cambridge University Press, 1988.

-----. "The Informer (An Ironic Tale)" (1908). In: *Joseph Conrad: Selected Short Stories*. Ware: Wordsworth Classics, 1997.

Joyce, James. *Stephen Hero* (1944). Ed. Theodore Spencer, Norfolk, CN: New Directions, 1963.

Lawrence, D.H. *Women in Love* (1920). The Definitive Text. The Cambridge Edition of the Works of D.H. Lawrence. Ed. David Farmer *et al*. London: Grafton Books, 1988.

-----. *The Collected Letters of D.H. Lawrence*. Vol.I and II. Ed. Harry T. Moore. London: Heinemann, 1962.

-----. *The Letters of D.H. Lawrence: Volume II, June 1913-October 1916*. The Cambridge Edition of the Letters of D.H. Lawrence. Eds. George J. Zytaruk, James T. Boulton. Cambridge: Cambridge University Press, 2002.

-----. *The Prussian Officer and Other Stories* (1914). The Cambridge Edition of the Works of D.H. Lawrence. Ed. John Worthen. London: Panther Books, 1985.

-----. *The Rainbow* (1915). London: Penguin, 2000.

Lewis, Percy Wyndham. *Tarr* (1918). The 1918 Version. Ed. Paul O'Keeffe. Santa Rossa: Black Sparrow Press, 1996.

-----. *Blasting and Bombardiering* (1937). London: John Calder, 1982.

-----. *Rude Assignment* (1950). London: Hutchinson, 1950.

-----. *Tarr* (1928). Ed. Scott W. Klein. Oxford: Oxford University Press, 2010.

-----. *The Complete Wild Body* (1927). Ed. Bernard Lafourcade. Santa Barbara: Black Sparrow Press, 1982.

-----. *The Letters of Wyndham Lewis.* Ed. W.K. Rose. London: Methuen, 1963.

General Background

Ardis, Ann L. *Modernism and Cultural Conflict, 1880-1922.* Cambridge: Cambridge University Press, 2002.

-----. *New Women, New Novels: Feminism and Early Modernism.* New Brunswick: Rutgers University Press, 1990.

Arendt, Hannah. *On Violence.* London: Harcourt Brace & Company, 1970.

Bailie, Gil. *Violence Unveiled: Humanity at the Crossroads.* New York: The Crossroads Publishing Company, 1997.

Benjamin, Walter. *Illuminations: Essays and Reflections.* Ed. Hannah Arendt. Trans. Harry Zohn. New York: Shocken Books, 1985.

-----. *Reflections: Essays, Aphorisms, Autobiographical Writings.* Ed. Peter Demetz. Trans. Edmund Jephcott. New York: Shocken Books, 1986.

Bernhardi, Friedrich von. *Germany and the Next War* (1912). Trans. Allen H. Powles. Honolulu: University Press of the Pacific, 2001.

Bloom, Clive, ed. *Literature and Culture in Modern Britain: Volume I, 1900-1929.* London: Longman, 1993.

Booth, Allyson. *Postcards from the Trenches: Negotiating the Space between Modernism and the First World War.* Oxford: Oxford University Press, 1996.

Bourke, Joanna. *Dismembering the Male: Men's Bodies, Britain and the Great War.* London: Reaktion Books, 1996.

Bradbury, Malcolm, McFarlane, James, eds. *Modernism: A Guide to European Literature, 1890-1930.* London: Penguin, 1991.

Carey, John. *The Intellectuals and the Masses: Pride and Prejudice among the Literary Intelligentsia, 1880-1939.* London: Faber, 1992.

Carr, Steven Alan, "Mass Murder, Modernity and the Alienated Gaze." In: Murray, Pomerance, ed. *Cinema and Modernity*. New Brunswick: Rutgers University Press, 2006. 57-73.

Catteau, Jacques. *Dostoevsky and the Process of Literary Creation*. Trans. Audrey Littlewood. Cambridge: Cambridge University Press, 1989.

Childs, Peter. *Modernism*. London: Routledge, 2000.

Cohen, Milton A. "Fatal Symbiosis: Modernism and the First World War." In: Quinn, Patrick J., Trout, Steven, eds. *The Literature of the Great War Reconsidered: Beyond Modern Memory*. London: Palgrave Macmillan, 2001. 159-171.

Conrad, Peter. *Modern Times, Modern Places: How Life and Art Were Transformed in a Century of Revolution, Innovation, and Radical Change*. London: Thames and Hudson, 1998.

Dyer, Geoff. *The Missing of the Somme*. London: Hamish Hamilton, 1994.

Eagleton, Terry. *Holy Terror*. Oxford: Oxford University Press, 2005.

-----. *Sweet Violence: The Idea of the Tragic*. Oxford: Blackwell Publishing, 2003.

Eksteins, Modris. *Rites of Spring: The Great War and the Birth of the Modern Age*. London: Black Swan, 1989.

Ferall, Charles. *Modernist Writing and Reactionary Politics*. Cambridge: Cambridge University Press, 2001.

Frazer, James, Sir. *The Golden Bough* (1922). London: Touchstone, 1995.

Fussel, Paul. *The Great War and Modern Memory*. Oxford: Oxford University Press, 1975.

Giddens, Anthony, ed. *Emile Durkheim: Selected Writings*. Cambridge: Cambridge University Press, 1972.

-----. *The Nation State and Violence: Volume Two of a Contemporary Critique of Historical Materialism*. Berkeley: University of California Press, 1987.

Girard, René. *Deceit, Desire and the Novel: Self and Other in Literature*. Trans. Yvonne Freccero. Baltimore: The Johns Hopkins University Press, 1961.

-----. *The Scapegoat*. Trans. Yvonne Freccero. Baltimore: The Johns Hopkins University Press, 1986.

-----. *To Double Business Bound: Essays on Literature, Mimesis and Anthropology*. Baltimore: The Johns Hopkins University Press, 1988.

-----. *Things Hidden Since the Foundation of the World*. Research Undertaken in Collaboration with Jean-Michel Oghourlian and Guy Lefort. Trans. Stephen Bann (Books I and III) and Michael Metteer (Book II). London: The Athlone Press, 1987.

-----. *Violence and the Sacred*. Trans. Patrick Gregory. London, The Athlone Press, 1995.

Hamerton-Kelly, Robert, ed. *Violent Origins: Walter Burkert, René Girard and Jonathan Z. Smith on Ritual Killing and Cultural Formation*. Stanford: Stanford University Press, 1987.

Hoffman, Piotr. *Violence in Modern Philosophy*. Chicago: University of Chicago Press, 1989.

Horsley, Lee. *The Noir Thriller*. London: Palgrave, 2001.

Houen, Alan. *Terrorism in Modern Literature: From Joseph Conrad to Ciaran Carson.* Oxford: Oxford University Press, 2002.

Hynes, Samuel. *A War Imagined: The First World War and English Culture.* London: Pimlico, 1992.

Jameson, Fredric. *The Political Unconscious: Narrative as a Socially Symbolic Act.* London: Methuen, 1981.

Johnsen, William A. *Violence and Modernism: Ibsen, Joyce and Woolf.* Gainessville: University Press of Florida, 2003.

Kasinitz, Philip, ed. *Metropolis: Center and Symbol of Our Times.* London: Macmillan, 1995.

Kaye, Peter. *Dostoevsky and English Modernism, 1900-1930.* Cambridge: Cambridge University Press, 1999.

Lawrence, Philip K. *Modernity and War: The Creed of Absolute Violence.* London: Palgrave Macmillan, 1997.

Levenson, Michael. *Modernism and the Fate of Individuality: Character and Novelistic Form from Conrad to Woolf.* Cambridge: Cambridge University Press, 1991.

-----, ed. *The Cambridge Companion to Modernism.* Cambridge: Cambridge University Press, 1999.

Nicholls, Peter. *Modernisms: A Literary Guide.* London: Macmillan, 1995.

Nietzsche, Friedrich. *Thus Spoke Zarathustra* (1885). Cambridge Texts in the History of Philosophy. Eds. Robert Pippin *et al.* Cambridge: Cambridge University Press, 2006.

Nordau, Max Simon. *The Conventional Lies of Our Civilisation* (1895). Charleston: BiblioBazaar, 2010.

Philips, W.M. *Landscapes of Anarchy: Language and Cultural Change, 1870-1914.* Lewisburg: Bucknell University Press, 2003.

Poplawski, Paul, ed. *Encyclopaedia of Literary Modernism.* Westport: Greenwood Press, 2003.

Redding, Arthur F. *Raids on Human Consciousness: Writing, Anarchism, and Violence.* Columbia: University of South Carolina Press, 1998.

Roth, Jack J. *The Cult of Violence: Sorel and the Sorelians.* London: University of California Press, 1980.

Sheehan, Paul. *Modernism, Narrative and Humanism.* Cambridge: Cambridge University Press, 2002.

Smith, Andrew; Wallace, Jeff, eds. *Gothic Modernisms.* London: Palgrave, 2001.

Sorel, Georges, *Reflections on Violence* (1908). Ed. Jeremy Jennings. Cambridge: Cambridge University Press, 1999.

Stamirowska, Krystyna, ed. *Historia, fikcja, (auto)biografia w powieści brytyjskiej XX wieku,* Kraków: Universitas, 2006.

Stanage, Sherman, ed. *Reason and Violence: Philosophical Investigations.* Oxford: Basil Blackwell, 1974.

Stevenson, Randall. *Modernist Fiction*. Revised edition. London, Prentice Hall, 1998.

Stone, Dan. *Breeding Superman: Nietzsche, Race and Eugenics in Edwardian and Interwar Britain*. Liverpool: Liverpool University Press, 2002.

Szakolczai, Arpad. "Civilization and Its Sources," *International Sociology*, Vol.16:3, 2001. 369-386.

Tate, Trudi. *Modernism, History and the First World War*. Manchester: Manchester University Press, 1998.

Trotter, David. *Paranoid Modernism: Literary Experiment, Psychosis, and the Professionalization of English Society*. Oxford: Oxford University Press, 2001.

-----. *The English Novel in History, 1985-1920*. London: Routledge, 1993.

Webb, Eugene. "René Girard: Consciousness and the Dynamics of Desire." In: *Philosophers of Consciousness: Polanyi, Lonergan, Voegelin, Ricoeur, Girard, Kierkegaard*. Seattle: University of Washington Press, 1988.

Weir, David. *Anarchy and Culture: The Aesthetic Politics of Modernism*. Amherst: University of Massachusetts Press, 1997.

Whitmer, Barbara. *The Violence Mythos*. New York: State University of New York Press, 1997.

Williams, Louise Blakeney. *Modernism and the Ideology of History: Literature, Politics, and the Past*. Cambridge: Cambridge University Press, 2002.

Internet Sources

Ken Newton, University of Dundee. "Women in Love." In: Clark, Robert, ed. *The Literary Encyclopedia*. 1 Nov. 2002. The Literary Dictionary Company. 24 June 2005. <http://www.litencyc.com/php/sworks.php?rec=true&UID=8853>

"Viking warriors. The Berserker." The Viking History Theme Page. Retrieved 1 Dec. 2003. <http://www.stemnet.nf.ca/CITE/v_berserker.htm>

Criticism of Joseph Conrad

Ash, Sharon Beth. *Writing in Between: Modernity and Psychological Dilemma in the Novels of Joseph Conrad*. New York: St. Martin's Press, 1999.

Bernstein, Stephen. "Politics, Modernity, and Domesticity: The Gothicism of Conrad's *The Secret Agent*." *CLIO*, Vol.32, 2003.

Berthoud, Jacques. *Joseph Conrad: The Major Phase*. Cambridge: Cambridge University Press, 1979.

Cooper, Christopher. *Conrad and the Human Dilemma*. London: Chatto & Windus, 1970.

Coroneos, Con. "Conrad, Kropotkin and Anarchist Geography." *The Conradian, Journal of the Joseph Conrad Society*. 18:2. 1994. 15-31.

-----. *Space, Conrad and Modernity*. Oxford: Oxford University Press, 2002.

Daleski, H.M. *Joseph Conrad: The Way of Dispossession*. London: Faber and Faber, 1977.

Darras, Jacques. *Joseph Conrad and the West: Signs of Empire*. Trans. Anne Luyat and Jacques Darras. London: Macmillan, 1982.

Fleishman, Avrom. *Conrad's Politics: Community and Anarchy in the Fiction of Joseph Conrad*. Baltimore: The Johns Hopkins Press, 1967.

-----. "The Landscape of Hysteria in *The Secret Agent*." In: Murfin, Ross C., ed. *Conrad Revisited: Conrad for the Eighties*. Alabama: University of Alabama Press, 1985. 89-105.

Gekoski, R.A. *Conrad: The Moral World of the Novelist*. London: Paul Elek, 1978.

Guerard, Albert J. *Conrad the Novelist*. New York: Atheneum, 1970.

Hamilton, Carol Vanderveer. "Revolution from within: Conrad's natural anarchists." *The Conradian, Journal of the Joseph Conrad Society*. Vol.18:2. 1994. 31-49.

Hawthorn, Jeremy. *Joseph Conrad: Narrative Technique and Ideological Commitment*. London: Edward Arnold, 1990.

Hervouet, Yves. *The French Face of Joseph Conrad*. Cambridge: Cambridge University Press, 1990.

Hollywood, Paul. "Conrad and Anarchist Theories of Language." In: Carabine, Keith; Knowles, Owen; Krajka, Wiesław, eds. *Contexts for Conrad*. Lublin: Maria Curie-Skłodowska University, 1993. 243-264.

Hunter, Allan. *Joseph Conrad and the Ethics of Darwinism*. London and Canberra: Croom Helm, 1983.

Johnson, Bruce. *Conrad's Models of Mind*. Minneapolis: University of Minnesota Press, 1971.

Jordan, Elaine, ed. *Joseph Conrad: Contemporary Critical Essays*. London: Macmillan, 1996.

Kaplan, Carola M. *et al. Conrad in the Twenty-First Century: Contemporary Approaches and Perspectives*. London: Routledge, 2005.

Knowles, Owen; Moore, Gene M. *Oxford Reader's Companion to Conrad*. Oxford: Oxford University Press, 2000.

Land, Stephen K. *Conrad and the Paradox of the Plot*. London: Macmillan, 1984.

Mann, Thomas. "Conrad's *The Secret Agent*" (first published as an Introduction to the German translation of *The Secret Agent* in 1926). In: R.W. Stallman, ed. *The Art of Joseph Conrad: A Critical Symposium*. East Lansing: Michigan University Press, 1960. 227-234.

McMaster, Graham, "Some Other Secrets in *The Secret Agent*." In: *Literature and History*, Manchester University Press, 12:2. 1986. 229-242.

Moore, Gene M., ed. *Conrad's Cities: Essays for Hans van Marle*. Amsterdam and Atlanta: Rodopi, 1992.

Morf, Gustav. *The Polish Shades and Ghosts of Joseph Conrad*. New York: Astra Books, 1976.

Mulry, David. "Popular Accounts of the Greenwich Bombing and Conrad's *The Secret Agent.*" *Rocky Mountain Review.* Washington University Press. (Fall 2000). 43-64.

Najder, Zdzisław, ed. *Conrad w oczach krytyki światowej.* Warszawa: Państwowy Instytut Wydawniczy, 1974.

-----. *Joseph Conrad.* New Brunswick: Rutgers University Press, 1983.

Ray, Martin. "Conrad, Nordau and Other Degenerates: The Psychology of *The Secret Agent.*" *Conradiana.* 16. 1984. 125-40.

Reilly, Jim. *Shadowtime: History and Representation in Hardy, Conrad and George Eliot.* London: Routledge, 1994.

Rieselbach, Helen Funk. *Conrad's Rebels: The Psychology of Revolution in the Novels from Nostromo to Victory.* Michigan: UMI Research Press, Ann Arbor, 1985.

Rosenfield, Claire. *Paradise of Snakes: An Archetypal Analysis of Conrad's Political Works.* Chicago: University of Chicago Press, 1967.

Roussel, Royal. *The Metaphysics of Darkness: A Study in the Unity and Development in Conrad's Fiction.* Baltimore and London: The Johns Hopkins Press, 1971.

Said, Edward W. "Conrad and Nietzsche." In: Sherry, Norman, ed. *Joseph Conrad: A Commemoration.* Papers from the 1974 International Conference on Conrad. London: Macmillan, 1976. 65-76.

Saveson, J.E. *Conrad the Late Moralist.* Amsterdam: Rodopi N.V., 1974.

Schwarz, Daniel R. *Conrad: Almayer's Folly to Under Western Eyes.* London: Macmillan, 1980.

Shaffer, Brian W. "The London Fog: Civilization as Rhetoric and Game in Conrad." In: *The Blinding Torch: Modern British Fiction and the Discourse of Civilization.* Amherst: University of Massachusetts Press, 1993. 63-78.

Sherry, Norman. *Conrad's Western World.* Cambridge: Cambridge University Press, 1971.

Spittles, Brian. *Joseph Conrad: Text and Context.* London: Macmillan, 1992.

Stape, J.H., ed. *The Cambridge Companion to Joseph Conrad.* Cambridge: Cambridge University Press, 1996.

Stine, Peter. "Conrad's Secrets in *The Secret Agent,*" *Conradiana.* 13:2. 1981. 123-140.

Sypher, Eileen. "Anarchism and Gender: James's *The Princess Casamassima* and Conrad's *The Secret Agent.*" *Henry James Review.* 9:1. 1998. 1-16.

Watt, Ian. "The Political and Social Background of *The Secret Agent.*" In: Watt, Ian. *Essays on Conrad.* Cambridge: Cambridge University Press, 2000. 112-125.

Criticism of Wyndham Lewis

Ayers, David. *Wyndham Lewis and Western Man.* London: Macmillan, 1992.

Brown, Dennis. *Intertextual Dynamics within the Literary Group—Joyce, Lewis, Pound and Eliot. The Men of 1914.* London: Macmillan, 1990.

Campbell, Sue Ellen. "The Enemy Attacks: Wyndham Lewis versus Ezra Pound." *Journal of Modern Literature*. 10:2. 1983. 247-257.

-----. *The Enemy Opposite: The Outlaw Criticism of Wyndham Lewis*. Athens: Ohio University Press, 1986.

Corbett, David Peters, ed. *Wyndham Lewis and the Art of Modern War*. Cambridge: Cambridge University Press, 1998.

Edwards, Paul. *Wyndham Lewis: Painter and Writer*. New Haven and London: Paul Mellon Centre for Studies in British Art, Yale University Press, 2000.

Foshay, Toby Avard. *Wyndham Lewis and the Avant-Garde: The Politics of the Intellect*. Montreal, London: McGill-Queen's University Press, 1992.

Gąsiorek, Andrzej. "'The Cave-Men of the New Mental Wilderness': Wyndham Lewis and the Self in Modernity." *Wyndham Lewis Annual*, 1999. 3-20.

-----. *Wyndham Lewis and Modernism*. Horndon, Tavistock: Northcote (Writers and Their Work), 2004.

Jameson, Fredric. *Fables of Aggression: Wyndham Lewis, the Modernist as Fascist*. Berkeley: University of California Press, 1979.

Kenner, Hugh. *Wyndham Lewis*. Norfolk: New Directions, 1954.

Kush, Thomas. *Wyndham Lewis's Pictorial Integer*. Michigan: UMI Research Press, 1981.

Materer, Timothy. *Vortex: Pound, Eliot and Lewis*. London: Cornell University Press, 1979.

-----. *Wyndham Lewis, the Novelist*. Detroit: Wayne State University Press, 1976.

Meyers, Jeffrey, ed. *Wyndham Lewis: A Revaluation*. London: Athlone Press, 1980.

Munton, Alan. "'Imputing Noxiousness': Aggression and Mutilation in Recent Lewis Criticism." *Wyndham Lewis Annual*, 1997. 5-19.

-----. "Fantasies of Violence: The Consequences of Not Reading Wyndham Lewis." *Wyndham Lewis Annual*, 1998. 31-49.

O'Keeffe, Paul. *Some Sort of Genius: A Life of Wyndham Lewis*. London: Jonathan Cape, 2000.

Peppis, Paul. "Anti-Individualism and the Fictions of National Character in Wyndham Lewis's *Tarr*." *Twentieth Century Literature*. 40:2. 1994. 226-255.

-----. *Literature, Politics, and the English Avant-garde: Nation and Empire, 1901-1918*. Cambridge: Cambridge University Press, 2000.

Schenker, Daniel. *Wyndham Lewis: Religion and Modernism*. Tuscaloosa and London: The University of Alabama Press, 1992.

Symons, Julian, ed. *The Essential Wyndham Lewis: An Introduction to His Work*. London: Vintage, 1991.

Criticism of D.H. Lawrence

Aldritt, Keith. *The Visual Imagination of D.H. Lawrence*. London: Edward Arnold, 1971.

Becket, Fiona. *The Complete Critical Guide to D.H. Lawrence*. London: Routledge, 2002.

Black, Michael, ed. *D.H. Lawrence: The Early Philosophical Works*. Cambridge: Cambridge University Press, 1992.

Bradshaw, David, ed. Introduction to *Women in Love*. Oxford: Oxford University Press, 1998. xviii-xxxviii.

Casey, Simon. *Naked Liberty and the World of Desire: Elements of Anarchism in the Work of D.H. Lawrence*. London: Routledge, 2003.

Clarke, Bruce. "D.H. Lawrence and the *Egoist* Group." *Journal of Modern Literature*. XVIII:1. 1992. 65-76.

Clarke, Colin, ed. *D.H. Lawrence:* The Rainbow *and* Women in Love. London: Macmillan, 1978.

Doherty, Gerald. *Theorising Lawrence: Nine Meditations on Tropological Themes*. New York: Peter Lang, 1999.

Draper, R.P. *D.H. Lawrence: The Critical Heritage*. London: Routledge, 1997.

Fernihough, Anne. *D.H. Lawrence: Aesthetics and Ideology*. Oxford: Clarendon, 1993.

Gomme, Andor Harvey. *D.H. Lawrence: A Critical Study of the Major Novels and Other Writings*. New York: Barnes and Noble, 1978.

Harrison, Andrew. *D.H. Lawrence and Italian Futurism: A Study of Influence*. Amsterdam: Rodopi B.V., 2003.

Hough, Graham. *The Dark Sun: A Study of D.H. Lawrence*. London: Gerald Duckworth, 1956.

Kalnis, Maria, ed. *D.H. Lawrence: Centenary Essays*. Bristol: Bristol Classical Press, 1986.

Leavis, Frank Raymond *D.H. Lawrence: Novelist*. London: Pelican, 1978.

Meyers, Jeffrey, ed. *D.H. Lawrence and Tradition*. Amherst: The University of Massachusetts Press, 1985.

Milton, Colin. *Lawrence and Nietzsche: a Study in Influence*. Aberdeen: Aberdeen University Press, 1987.

Montgomery, Robert E. *The Visionary D.H. Lawrence: Beyond Philosophy and Art*. Cambridge: Cambridge University Press, 1994.

Poplawski, Paul. *D.H. Lawrence: A Reference Companion*. Westport: Greenwood Press, 1996.

Pritchard, R.E. *D.H. Lawrence: Body of Darkness*. London: Hutchinson, 1971.

Ross, Charles L. *Women in Love: A Novel of Mythic Realism*. Boston: Twayne Publishers, 1991.

Sagar, Keith. *The Art of D.H. Lawrence*. Cambridge: Cambridge University Press, 1966.

Seligmann, Herbert J. *D.H. Lawrence: An American Interpretation*. New York: T. Seltzer, 1924.

Steinberg, Erwin R. "D.H.Lawrence: Mythographer." *Journal of Modern Literature*, XXV:1, 2001. 91-108.

Stewart, Jack F. "The Myth of the Fall in *Women in Love.*" *Philological Quarterly.* 74:4. 1995. 443-451.

------. *The Vital Art of D.H. Lawrence: Vision and Expression.* Carbondale: Southern Illinois University Press, 1999.

Templeton, Wayne. *States of Estrangement: The Novels of D.H. Lawrence, 1912-1917.* Troy: The Whiston Publishing Company, 1989.

Walterscheid, Kathryn A. *The Resurection of the Body: Touch in D.H. Lawrence.* New York: Peter Lang, 1993.

Widmer, Kingsley. *Defiant Desire: Some Dialectical Legacies of D.H. Lawrence.* Carbondale: Southern Illinois University Press, 1992.

Worthen, John. *D.H. Lawrence.* London: Edward Arnold, 1991.

-----. *D.H. Lawrence: The Early Years, 1885-1930.* Cambridge: Cambridge University Press, 1992.

Wussow, Helen. *The Nightmare of History: The Fictions of Virginia Woolf and D.H. Lawrence.* Betlehem: Lehigh University Press, London: Associated University Press, 1998.